Divine Threads Within A Human Tapestry

Memoirs of

Phil Parshall

William Carey Library
Pasadena, California

William Carey Library
P.O. Box 40129
Pasadena, CA 91114
(626) 798-0819

Library of Congress and Cataloging-in-Publication Data
Parshall, Phil
Divine threads within a human tapestry :
memoirs of Phil Parshall / Phil Parshall. p. cm.
ISBN 0-87808-602-1
(pbk. : alk. paper)

1. Parshall, Phil. 2.Missionaries--Bangladesh--Biography. 3. Missionaries--
Philippines--Biography. 4. Missionaries--United States--Biography. 5. Missions
to Muslims. I. Title.

BV2626.P37 A3 2000
266'.0092--dc21
[B]
00-060882

Cover design by Mary Lou Totten

Printed in the United States of America

6 5 4 3 2 1
04 03 02 01 00

Julie

Skilled weaver who, second only to Jesus Christ,
has brought together my tapestry into a
cohesiveness and wholeness.
No words are adequate to express my devotedness to you as a
person, lover, and friend.

Lyndi and David Thomas
Ian Philip and Jacqueline Rose

With deepest love and appreciation
for a terrific daughter, son-in-law, grandson,
and granddaughter.

Other books by the author:

The Fortress and the Fire

New Paths In Muslim Evangelism

Bridges to Islam

Beyond the Mosque

The Cross and the Crescent

Inside the Community

The Last Great Frontier

Contents

Foreword

"Phil, you must write a book." I have often said this to my dear friend, who has touched my life deeply. And others who have walked through the emotional word pictures painted in Phil and Julie Parshall's letters over the years have said that repeatedly. He did, of course, write seven fascinating and unusual books to help Christians reach out to the Muslim world, and we rejoice in those invaluable resources. But that was not what we meant!

Here Phil has shared the joys and sorrows of thirty-nine years of service in Asia, a personal, intimate look into the life of a missionary who has "been there, done that," but still retains a questing mind, insatiable curiosity, and keen grasp of the issues.

Hurt, but not stopped by what would now be called a dysfunctional childhood and upbringing, Phil has disdained to sugarcoat his failures, struggles, and rough edges. An astute observer who feels deeply and writes with a pen of fire, he has given us pathos without sentimentality, and has shared with candor the joy and accomplishments of missionary life on the cutting edge.

And life is never dull around the Parshall household. This work makes the reader eyewitness to the rise and fall of governments, careers, and hopes. Declaring his intent to show his life as a weaving of God's tapestry, Phil has done some weaving of his own, at appropriate places stating his values and his philosophy of missions. He talks of issues like temptation, the meaning of true spirituality, sacrifice, suffering, and dedication.

The free-wheeling style of this book will give English teachers pause, and its probing thoughtfulness will put theologians on the defensive. But the uninhibited honesty and zest for life with which

Phil writes will keep every reader turning the pages. Now, Phil, that is what we meant!

Ed Welch, Associate Personnel Director
SIM USA

Now here is a story! Unlike his other books on Islamic subjects, this is the compelling human drama of Phil and Julie Parshall's lives. It is a warm, powerful, inspiring story.

Phil's conversion was simply life-changing. Then Phil was propelled from a difficult life with his dysfunctional family to studying at several colleges and universities. Among them were the Fuller School of World Mission, Wheaton Graduate School, and Harvard University.

After completing their graduate studies, Phil and Julie transferred their skills to distant lands. What is it like to set up housekeeping without electricity in a rural village in poverty-stricken Bangladesh? How does is feel to move to the capital city of that land and be offered the home of the nation's president for your burgeoning Bible Correspondence school? What goes through your mind as you operate an outreach center in a difficult and dangerous Muslim neighborhood in Manila, Philippines? This book answers these questions, and in it Phil asks many of his own probing, mind-bending queries. Some he answers and others he leaves for you to grapple with.

The Parshall story is remarkably candid. No sugar-coating here. Phil tells of his weaknesses, deepest disappointments, and times of despair in a way that makes us feel them with him. Then he relates joys and victories that lift our spirits along with his own.

We come to know and appreciate his Julie, his gem. She is the loving, stable, steady, counterpoint to Phil's sometimes mercurial disposition. We say to ourselves, "What would he have done without her?"

Read *Divine Threads Within a Human Tapestry* and get to know Phil and Julie intimately. They are both trained, experienced, effective, spiritually minded, courageous lovers of Muslim people around the world. Phil shines forth as a scholar, teacher, author, and statesman who continues today in the thick of the battle. And, as you read, you will see the divine threads glimmering through the tapestry of two unique and very appealing lives. Don't miss this!

Viggo B. Olsen, M.D., Litt.D., D.H. Founder of Memorial Christian Hospital in Bangladesh and author of *Daktar/Dipolomat in Bangladesh*

Introduction

It has been said that the writing of one's memoirs is like a rite of exorcism of the demons within, a venting of repressed emotional trauma. Letting all "hang out" is supposedly good for the soul.

So perhaps that is what the following pages are all about. Certainly I have felt a measure of release in allowing my memory to slowly cruise back through the decades. Hindsight lends a much better perspective than trying to analyze an ongoing situation in which we find ourselves immersed.

There is more. I am always on the lookout for the formation of a design within the tapestry. What goes where? Why? Where are all of these diverse threads heading? Is there a symmetry evolving? And finally, is the end result worth all of the effort? That, to me, encapsulates the riddle of life that I will pursue with vigor until, at last, my faculties of reason are beyond utilization.

These following reflections are a rather frank chronicle of my pilgrimage of quest. It has not always been an easy journey. A few readers may be shocked by my honesty. So be it. One of my greater irritations in life is to be subjected to whitewashed biographies. They are of no real help to those of us who are robed in sinful flesh and who are utterly committed to rising up after each fall and pressing on. It is in this spirit that I write with the great hope that other strugglers may realize they are not alone on their journey of life.

In certain of the situations described, I have felt it best to use pseudonyms. Then, there are a number of hurting episodes I have intentionally omitted. I have no desire to embarrass or offend anyone. By far, the greatest problem in my life is self, not others.

So many saints have been such an encouragement. It is impossible to recognize them all in this book. But I am deeply grateful for each one who has assisted me on my pilgrimage, especially for my closest male friend, Ed Welch, for his *Foreword*, as well as his meticulous editing of my writings.

A central motif of these reflections is the tapestry. My thanks to Betty King who has allowed me to share her musings.

> *A tapestry is a beautiful work of art, one that is created by a skillful designer. Its loveliness is reflected in the various threads of color as each one, with its own shading and hue, is placed individually within the pattern. A pattern that was conceived from the beginning and dimensions that were set at the start will one day emerge as a completed work.*
>
> *The story of the individual life is like the unfolding display of a tapestry. Created and fashioned by God, each person has God-ordained dimensions of living and purpose. Each experience is like the colorful threads, placed stitch by stitch, with their own highlights of richness and intensity—some are vibrant and others somber. As one is taught the necessary lessons of life, blending occurs.*
>
> *With the giving of our gifts and use of our talents, we grow in increasing maturity and reflect a more wondrous display of the grace and sovereignty of God.*

Chapter 1

Family

Waves of envy would wash over my emotions as I observed friends run gleefully to their dads and enfold themselves in strong arms of love. Oh, for a father I could admire and respect. In my memory bank I cannot find a moment of intimacy with my dad. Rather, this man who shared a dwelling with Mom, my older brother, and myself, was, to me, an object of piercing shame.

Dad was an only son, loved and overly protected by a doting mother while concurrently being constantly harassed and belittled by a disgusted father. Torn between intense emotional reactions, Dad evolved into a societal misfit. He was strange. Not violent, but just out of sync with life, with people, and with God.

His father was a modestly successful businessman with his own machine shop in Fort Myers, Florida. My grandfather was always proud to tell all who would listen about his relationship with Thomas Edison, who would, from time to time, send work to his shop. My sanguine grandmother derived even greater joy relating her stories about playing bridge with Mrs. Edison. These high points of life would occur when the Edisons visited their winter home each year in Fort Myers.

This grandfather was a positive role model to me during my youth. He was respected in the community and he even once considered running for mayor. By temperament he was introverted. In his mid-40's he was reputed to have suffered a nervous breakdown. Despite smoking cigars constantly and drinking straight whiskey in unbelievable quantities (which he held very well), Granddad, to me, was someone to respect, though not particularly to love. I have no recollection of an embrace from this man.

Dad was a welder, and an excellent one, "Actually one of the best in the country,"—or so he frequently reminded me. Perhaps this was his way of reaching out and pursuing the respect that he knew I was withholding. From my earliest childhood until I was 13 years old, Dad worked at my grandfather's machine shop. This simply was a disaster. Being the boss's son meant, to my dad, that slothfulness in work was a birthright. Not so to Granddad! The emotional eruptions were volcanic in intensity. Dad's refuge was found in a local bar where there was always a half-drunken reject who would nod sympathetically to repeated stories of real or imagined parental abuse.

Coming home each evening, Dad would enact a repetitive scenario of joy and anger. Walking through the door would be a whistling, happy person. Rather thin and not particularly handsome, Dad would engage in small talk. But suddenly, a word or a look from Mom or one of us boys, or perhaps an unpleasant memory from the day would invade a brain quadrant. Without warning, curse words came gushing forth. Inwardly, and at times outwardly, I cringed. It was as if my nerve circuits were undergoing an overload surge. Within moments, Dad would be in the family's old jalopy, racing off into the setting sun. Back safely in the warm, accepting refuge of the bar Dad regained equilibrium. My most hurtful childhood recollection is that of screeching tires and a disappearing father. Never, never did I want to introduce my friends to "my dad."

Apart from temporary and superficial bar buddies, my father had no real friends. His erratic behavior was a barrier to any lasting relationship. Yet, he desperately craved social acceptance. In later years, he had no greater delight than to take me to his "friends": a welder here, a waitress there, or a childhood buddy. They would all tolerate our visit with an impatience totally uncomprehended by dad.

Was there another side to my father? I recall my tenth birthday. Dad had worked for weeks at the shop constructing a gym bar for me. On the big day Dad brought it home. Taking me to the back yard, he proudly turned over to me his labor of love. Thanking him superficially, I immediately turned my attention to a BB gun that my grandparents had given me. Within minutes I heard that horrid screech of tires.

Dad loved Mom. He would scream vulgarities, he would throw household items around the room, he would deprive Mom of necessities, but he never touched her in anger. Conversely, he had no higher joy than to sit and talk with her for hours as they chain-smoked and drank endless cups of coffee. Mom was his intimate friend and the only person who could somehow endure his eccentricities. There was a streak of romanticism in Dad that was reserved for his lifelong lover of over 50 years.

How can a borderline beggar be a compulsive giver? Dad straddled the line. He was frequently in a bar hitting up an acquaintance for five dollars so we could have supper. But he could well walk out of the bar and give half of it away to a panhandler whom he had never met before. Such were the ways of my dad.

Then there was Mom, also an only child. A mystical aura surrounded her childhood. We never discovered the full story. She would, with an air of finality, quash our queries with, "What is there to say? I grew up in Michigan with people who were not my parents and then came to Florida in my late teens, met your dad, and married him. That's it. Period." We could not intrude further into her private space.

And that is how Mom survived. She retreated often to her safe cocoon of privacy. It was a quiet place where she could seemingly tune out the harshness of the real life she endured.

I loved and respected Mom with an unbroken devotion from my birth to her death. Quiet and unassuming, she, too, made few friends in life, apart from her husband-lover. How tenaciously she labored through the decades as a licensed practical nurse. My most instilled memory is of her walking out the door dressed in her white uniform to go to the bus stand and travel across town to the hospital where she worked a 3-11 shift. Often tired and suffering from various ailments, Mom seldom complained about her lot in life. She was a Stoic in the best sense of the word.

Yes, there were a few proofs of her human frailties along the way. I well remember one sad night when I was around six years old. Dad evidently prompted Mom to take a few drinks, something she seldom did. A giddy intoxication took control of both their minds. Suddenly they walked into the dining room, opened the dish cupboard and, one by one and in turns, commenced throwing dishes across the kitchen and onto the wall above the sink. I can still hear the sound of broken glass intermixed with the silly laughter of two drunken parents. They were quite oblivious to the effect of their actions on two scared young children. The next morning my brother and I got up very early and swept the glass-littered floor.

Mom had a tendency to be stubborn. This personality trait was particularly difficult for my brother in later years. If an issue of disagreement was of sufficient magnitude, Mom would simply refuse to talk to my brother or his family. I never had such a problem. I was Mom's favorite.

Jimmy

That brings us to my brother, Jimmy, who is two years my senior. Jealously reigned. I really didn't like the guy. He was better looking than me, had more girl friends, was accomplished in sports, and had his own car two years before I got mine. He was a pain.

Jimmy looked upon me as a minor irritant in life. I regarded him as a Goliath-type challenge. Somehow this giant must fall, by any means, foul or fair. I bided my time, limiting my attacks to verbal excursions that would move him to the verge of instituting means of restraint against me through brute force. My power of analysis usually worked. Occasionally, bruises would appear on various parts of my body reminding me of the necessity to give Jimmy a bit more space.

A new dimension in our adversarial relationship was reached when I attained the ripe old age of 16. By working after school hours and on Saturdays, I was able to purchase a 15 year old 1938 Ford for the grand price of $200. What a car! It looked sleek with its stylish fender skirts and purple reflector lights. But, best of all, this car was a drag king. Very few upshots of the road could outdo me in the 100 yards between red lights.

Therein was the point of conflict with my brother. He also was a "dragger." His problem was inadequacy under the hood. He went through several cars seeking vainly to claim total and ultimate supremacy over his "baby brother." To no avail. Once I was leading him on a wild chase down a fairly remote road. He was close to my rear bumper. Moving up toward 70 mph, I tired of the sport and let off the accelerator. Jimmy, seeing that he was headed into my rear end, veered up an embankment and onto a rail track. In horror, I watched my brother struggle for control and finally, miraculously guide the car back onto the road.

Several other encounters relating to cars took place in those teen years. Once, in exasperation at some real or imagined fault of mine, Jimmy revved up his car and sped down a 40 foot driveway, slamming into the back of my car. Hearing the clash of metal and broken glass, I ran out of the house in time to see Jimmy reverse his car and, with front end heavily damaged, back down the driveway. My car's rear-end had the tiniest dent beneath the bumper.

Another time we were together in Jimmy's car with several girls. On this occasion we were racing through the suburban streets of Fort Myers with a good friend setting the pace in the lead car. A sharp curve proved too much for our vehicle's inertia and my brother's driving ability. Screams pierced the night air as the car did a 1¾ flip, landing on its side just inches from a deep canal. Fire flamed from the engine. Quickly we climbed through the windows and threw sand on the flames. Only scratches and bruised egos were sustained, although the words that emanated from the girl's parents were, and still are, memorable.

Mom and Dad settled the "religious question" at the time of marriage. Dad was a most nominal Episcopalian and Mom was an even more nominal Roman Catholic. Religion was not to be discussed or practiced. They pretty well kept to their view, at least until the very latter part of their lives. I cannot remember ever seeing them in church during my pre-conversion years. Dad's one and only theological statement, so often repeated, was, "There was only one perfect human being, and He was crucified."

My brother followed our parents' example. He was married in a civil ceremony. Years later, prior to his conversion, he and his family did attend an Episcopal church. My grandparents had a certain flavor of religious orientation that usually prompted them to attend a liberal, formalistic church on Sunday mornings. Granddad was a high level Mason. But I doubt the reality of Christ was present in their lives.

So then, what divine threads can I identify in my familial relationships? It would be my opinion that "common grace" was indeed at work in my early years of life. More specifics will be seen in the next chapter. But here a few examples will suffice.

From Dad I learned how to be a "lover for life." In the midst of all of his idiosyncrasies, there was a consistent thread of expressed love for Mom. He was not able to share that same warmth for his two sons, but at least we were both able to closely observe love's interaction at the most important level found among humans. To this day, Jimmy and I are incurable romantics toward our wives.

Mom taught me discipline, tenacity, and the value of hard work. Deeply imbedded into the very fabric of her life was a determination to keep on moving forward regardless of the cost or inconvenience. I can only speculate where I would be today without that example and the quiet exhortations that consistently flowed from her life.

Jimmy's contribution was to come later in life. He definitely inherited a great deal of Mom's stick-to-itiveness. His story will be interwoven in pages to come.

My grandfather was always exhorting me to be true to my word. "Never, never renege on a promise," was his way of encouraging me to be a person of integrity. Our daughter, Lyndi, has benefited repeatedly from my insistence that, no matter the cost, I will fulfill my word to her.

Probably the glimmer of religious influence in my childhood came from my cheerful grandmother. At some deep level of sub-consciousness, I absorbed some of her desire for God.

Can character traits be defined as divine threads? By all means. The Lord uses so many varied threads to put together a tapestry. For this I am indeed grateful.

Chapter 2

Growing Up

"Come on Fatty, get down and crawl through the drain pipe or we will beat you to a pulp." I looked up into the scowling faces of five ten-year-old future recruits for the Mafia. They talked tough and looked tough, thus my assumption was they *were* tough. I quickly surveyed the diameter of the pipe which ran under the driveway. My seven-year-old body was replete with protrusions usually reserved for the mid-life years. In my fertile imagination I could see a fire truck rushing to the scene with sirens blaring. Their task? To rescue a fat, hysterical little boy stuck in the middle of a drain pipe.

The options were really bad. But the absolute reality of the beating compared to the possibility of making it through the drain pipe led me to choose the latter. Down I went into the slough and slowly crawled on hands and knees through the pipe. I emerged on the other side sane of mind and filthy of body. It was a memorable moment in the life of a sensitive young kid.

Fat, really fat, I was! From earliest recollection until the age of 14, I was forced to endure the taunts of a world populated by the cruel and heartless. During those miserable years, I refused to have my picture taken. To my knowledge, the only picture that exists of me prior to college is one taken when I was nine months old.

As will be seen, this bombardment of my central nervous system was cumulative in effect. Life was a drag. Perhaps my love for children has been enhanced because of those early struggles. On the other hand, I have little patience for the really obese. All my life I have had to struggle to maintain a moderate weight. When I observe waddling Americans, especially in "all you can eat" restaurants, I want to go up to them and forcefully exhort them to get into the battle, suffer, deprive themselves, and evolve into something more akin to "God's image." An additional component to my conviction is geographically related. I have lived mostly in Asia where the poor do not have a choice to make in favor of gastronomical hedonism. Even the wealthy shun a lifestyle of obesity. Of interest to me is that this subject of intemperance is seldom, if ever, mentioned in American pulpits. I guess the guilty would be too numerous and overly obvious.

Fat little boys are seldom popular with their peers. They are often lonely, with no available support system. It was during those painful years I developed a highly introspective procedure that remains with me. Frequently during the day, I will relive my interaction with a person's words and deeds. This can lead to joy or sadness as the case may be. There is little neutrality in my dealing with life. Emotion is strong and, at times, overpowering. My eyes are constantly surveying, my mind evaluating, and my emotions responding. Such an interactive temperament knows soaring heights and unfathomable depths. The foundation was solidly laid in the formative years of youth. The fat little boy smiled at the taunts, all the while internally collapsing.

Most memorable were the wandering years. Dad's alienation with his father had escalated to an intolerable level. With increasing frequency, I was being commissioned to go over to Granddad's house and humbly request five dollars which would enable us to eat another simple meal. On one frightening occasion, I stood quivering in front of a very angry grandfather. Indelibly etched in my memory is a cinematic, slow motion replay, as this tall, powerful man pulls out a few dollar bills and throws them on the floor in front of me. Yelling vulgarities, he stomped out of my presence. His rage was not really directed toward me. But I was the nearby representative of one whom he had come to regard as a totally worthless, irredeemable, only child.

Stressful Wanderings

My Dad was a compulsive dreamer. Surely around the corner would be found fame and fortune. The number of his rejected "inventions" testified to the futility of his attaining the greatness that he so desired. But as he approached 40, he felt now was the time to cut the umbilical cord and launch out into the real world. After all, he was "one of the best welders in America," just waiting to be discovered.

Thirteen. The age of hormonal metamorphosis. At best, a transitional period of perplexity and insecurity in any boy. There we were, a nuclear family of four, packing up every item we possessed. It all fit into a dilapidated car. We set off... an optimistic father, an apprehensive mom, an adventurous brother... and myself feeling overwhelmed with emotional dissonance.

Palmetto is a short drive from Fort Myers. But far enough to give new hope, at least that is what Dad kept telling us. I enrolled in the eighth grade and tried out for the junior high football team. Amazing presumption that was! I huffed and puffed through the practice sessions and sat on the bench during the real games. Once, at the end of a game, the coach looked around, confident he had let all his "third stringers" play. He glanced at my downcast eyes and realized what a serious oversight he had made. In I went to play three or four minutes of real football. Thus forever ended my active sports career, at the ripe old age of 13.

Unexplained sexual drives began to emerge. "Unexplained" because no one other than my peers taught me of sexual realities. That was okay with me. This wasn't a subject parents would be interested in anyway, or so I thought.

I had heard that several of the ten-year-olds in our apartment building would go into the woods and secretly engage in sexual intercourse. Out of curiosity and awakening desires, I persuaded one of the boys to include me in the next orgy. On the fateful day I excitedly listened from an upstairs balcony as my friend proposed to the girls that they all take a trip to the woods. Forcefully, adamantly, the girls refused. This was the first of many thwarted opportunities to be sexually active throughout the decade preceding my marriage to

Julie. How grateful I am to the Lord for His wonderful preservation of my purity.

Meanwhile, my father was proving his skill, not at welding, but at relational alienation. The beckoning siren of the world quickly turned shrill and scary. Over the next two years, Dad would continually find a problem of earth-shaking dimensions with his supervisor. His response was totally predictable. Telling his employer to "shove it," he would mount his chariot, squeal his tires, and return to his lover, his cigarettes, and his coffee. It always amazed us that the world contained so many monsters who masqueraded as employers.

And the bills would be on a roll. I was convinced the postal system was demonically created for the sole purpose of delivering bad news. At times, the collectors would come to the door; once even with an official-looking summons. Jimmy and I fixed that guy. We slipped out the back door and let the air out of one of his tires. Another time I was with my brother driving downtown when two of the bad guys caught us at a traffic light. They demanded we disembark right then and there. What shame overwhelmed us as we gathered a few personal items from the jeep and began the long trek home, all the while cursing a dad who didn't meet the required payments on the vehicle.

Soon it was time to leave Palmetto, a small town whose light had dimmed. Surely the Tampa-St. Petersburg area would hold new promise of fortune and security. Checking out of school in the middle of the year was disconcerting. Dad's dreams were my nightmares. During the next year and a half we moved houses every time the bill collectors became overly zealous. Our house moves usually took place in the evening hours. The next day the collection Mafia cursed their gods and I'm sure, vowed to never, never again fall prey to a Parshall-type shyster.

There was one specially frightening afternoon. A knock on the door of our small, one-bedroom furnished apartment (always "furnished" so as to ensure mobility) revealed the gas meter collection agent. In the 50's there were meters with an attached reservoir where quarters could be deposited, which would then ensure a gas supply throughout the house. Early on, Dad had discovered how to pry open the top, thus allowing him to retrieve each quarter deposited. It was a great scam, at least so Dad thought.

Now, Mom and I faced the meter man at the screen door. With unbelievable composure, she let the collector in and quickly disappeared into the bedroom. I sat frozen in fear in the living room awaiting the collector's reappearance after he saw the empty meter box in the kitchen. I was sure he would be requesting the use of our phone to call the police. Instead, this gentleman of mercy simply said, "Sorry, I can't get the meter open. I will be back tomorrow with an instrument that will get me into it." With that he walked out.

In reality, a two year old could have penetrated that box. How gracious he was to give us a second chance. That night a chastened father hit up all his bar friends for an amount equal to three months of gas usage. He changed the bills into quarters and inserted them into the meter. Interestingly, the collector did not return the next day or for the next three months that we lived in that apartment. But I guarantee you, the right number of quarters were awaiting him when he did show up.

One does not often meet the elite in the type of bars my Dad frequented. From time to time, Dad's bar buddies would return to our apartment with him. A rather uncouth guy appeared one evening. With great enthusiasm, he told Dad how easy he could become a well-heeled "passer." This operation was super simple. Just take large denomination counterfeit bills and go around town making small purchases. The "change" would then be authentic currency. A generous percentage would go to Dad for his efforts. Amazingly, my father refused the offer. Some weeks later, Dad met his friend again. He had lost weight and was basically a nervous wreck. We were all glad that the lure of easy money had been rejected.

Schooling was a no fun proposition. My comings and going in mid-year were disruptive. Socially, I continued to be a misfit, not in small measure due to my obesity. Overweight, due not to a huge intake, but rather caused by an inordinate emphasis on candy bars and cookies. Mom was frequently working in the evenings so Dad would give me ten cents for a large Hershey's bar. That was my well-rounded supper. For several months I worked in a bakery washing pots and pans. A fringe benefit was having free access to all the pastry leftovers. My weight went ballistic.

One quiet evening, Mom and I were sitting together talking about what a crummy existence we were all enduring—hard work and almost no money for any type of fun times—a father I didn't like or respect, and a brother that was a drag. So is this what life is all about?

"Mom," I said, "maybe the best thing is to end it all and just commit suicide." Thus spoke a hurting and confused 14-year-old boy. Mom expressed surprise and dumped cold water on such an extreme thought. Actually it was just a passing idea, one that never really obsessed me.

So, what was Dad up to? We were living in a dump of a house right next to the railroad track. The whole place convulsed each time a train roared by. Dad had no job, but as usual, he had a dream brewing that would bring in great riches. He would go up to Georgia and get a high paying job with Lockheed Aircraft. So, on the appointed day, Dad left us and went on a Trailways bus for points north and the pot of gold that would surely be found at the end of the rainbow.

Mom faithfully worked her shift at the hospital. For several weeks we heard nothing from Dad. One day, Jimmy and I saw Mom returning from a "drive" with the delivery man of the local dry cleaning store. We hit the ceiling! "Dad may be odd, but that is no reason for developing another relationship," we forcefully communicated to Mom. That was the end of her philandering for the rest of her life, at least as far as we ever knew.

A month later, a chastised Dad, broke and weary, reappeared on the doorstep. The old familiar lifestyle patterns had accompanied him on his trek northward. After a few days work, there would always be someone to give Dad a "dirty look" or a demeaning comment. Most emphatically my father did not have to endure such violations of his personhood. "Shove it!" On to the next job… and soon the prodigal came back to lick his wounds in the arms of a woman uniquely created to express unconditional love.

Our two years of deep misery came to an end. Jimmy and I were farmed out to our grandparents while Mom and Dad sought to make a "new start" in Miami. I was in the tenth grade and Jimmy in the eleventh. We shared a bed in a small guest room in a most comfortable home in a stately, palm-tree-lined, peaceful suburb of Fort Myers.

Metamorphosis

Then it happened. The magic, mystical moment for which poets receive recognition and remuneration struck potently into the depths of my psyche. I fell in LOVE.

Susan was toothpick thin and talked unceasingly. But, amazingly, there was in the world a real live person of the opposite sex who would go out on a date with me. Immediately, food lost its compelling attractiveness. The pounds began falling off so rapidly that there was speculation as to what disease had invaded my body.

Overnight, light dispelled the darkness. Hues of brilliant colors seemed to replace the drabness of my existence. Yes, life was worth living. Friendships began to be formed that were psychologically reinforcing. For the next eight years, I was seldom without a girlfriend. Some (many?) were rather unspectacular, and I can only thank the Lord that the high level of emotional and physical attraction usually wore thin rather quickly. Then it was on to new pastures. Actually, I am grateful for the variety. This has always led me to realize there has never been anyone like my wife, Julie. My objective mental review of the many dating relationships I engaged in over those years absolutely confirms the wisdom of my ultimate and absolute choice of a lifetime partner.

How do grandparents in their 60's adjust their lives to somehow tolerate the activities of two heathen teen-age boys? With great admiration, I conclude they did so with remarkable equilibrium. Of course, Granddad's very frequent trips to the bathroom were a great help to him. That was where he kept his large selection of whiskey bottles in a cupboard. As for our grandmother, her basic propensity to defend the guilty (as she was always doing for Dad) kept her happily occupied standing between Granddad and two delinquents.

A downside to the year was the absence of my mother. Our ties went very deep. So, when the call came telling Jimmy and me to pull up stakes once again and go to Miami, I was more than ready for the transition, even though it meant a new school and the hassles of making new friends. Dad had been able to find a low paying job with tolerant supervisors. His drinking and mood swings continued. Mom's skills as a nurse were always in demand, so she experienced no problem in keeping employed.

My eleventh and twelfth grades were spent in the large and prestigious Miami Senior High School. Prestigious because we were frequently number one in the state in the football playoffs. That automatically made us the best high school in Florida. Alas, they had to attain such lofty accomplishments without my assistance. My eighth grade encounter with football would last me a lifetime.

Vividly, I recall my intense desire to be selected for membership in one of the "service clubs." These were pre-fraternity type elite groupings which were supposed to be others-oriented. In actual fact, they only contributed to snobbery and fleshly pursuits. That was just fine with me.

I had a good friend who agreed to sponsor me for membership in the least prestigious of all the clubs. At least I had a chance to get a foot in the door, no matter how minor league. The big day arrived when senior members of the clubs went around the classrooms and, in front of applauding peers, "tapped" their new members. In they walked.

Rejection.... Depression overwhelmed me. It was my senior year and last chance. Never mind that most of the other 750 members of my graduating class also were not in the inner circle of the clubs. Within the very core of my being was an intense drive for recognition and popularity.

Academic excellence was not my goal in high school. I came out about midway in class ratings. That was sufficient for me. There was no way I could ever understand algebra. Besides, what practical use would such a dumb coupling of letters and numbers ever be to me?

As I take a retrospective look back into my pre-conversion years, I can clearly find distinctive divine threads in the tapestry of life.

This has always been gratifying to me. Under my grandmother's influence, I had attended her rather liberal Episcopal church for some years in an on and off pattern. The youth group was, for me, a place of fellowship rather than spiritual formation. Communion offered real wine to be savored, albeit in such a small quantity. Being an altar boy and carrying the cross in procession while parishioners bowed as I passed down the aisle pandered my ego. Unfortunately, the cross I bore had almost no impact in my life.

While in Tampa, I periodically attended an Episcopal church. There I was urged to be a part of confirmation classes. This I did with no great regularity. Particularly dull were the church creeds I was told to memorize. As the big day of confirmation approached, the priest in charge exasperatedly asked if I was really serious about this major spiritual landmark in my life. Looking hurt that he should even ask such a question, I assured him of my utmost dedication to the church.

Such pomp and ceremony! The bishop himself conducted the confirmation service. It truly was a memorable moment of solemnity. To the church I was now a bona fide member of the body of Christ. I was touched; but still had no real grasp of any biblical teaching or spiritual reality.

During high school in Miami, Saturday nights were dedicated to the pursuit of fleshly conquests with attractive female classmates. There was never any sense of guilt concerning these acts of physical exploitation. After all, that is what all of the guys did. Monday morning talk was full of "how far did you get?" Actually, the stories told were more fancy than reality. Yet the attempts were serious. In the 50's girls knew how both to bait the line and then at the proper moment, to cut the line. Frustrated fellows compensated by relating embellished and colorful myths.

Between these Saturday and Monday events came Sunday. With amazing repetitiveness, I would drive all alone a significant distance to attend early church. Sitting, standing, kneeling, I would follow the prescribed forms of a devout worshipper. There was absolutely no cognitive encounter with Christian truth. But deep in the recesses of my innermost being was a restless soul waiting to be unleashed. The Master Designer was standing patiently nearby in the shadows.

Chapter 3

Conversion and College

Walking casually down the corridor of Miami High one Thursday morning in March of 1955, I never could have dreamed a drama was about to unfold in the next twelve hours that would totally turn my world upside down. A girl of my acquaintance rather flippantly approached me and said, "Phil, there is going to be a cook-out tonight with lots of fellows and gals. Doesn't cost anything. Try and make it. Here's the address." With that, she melted into a rowdy crowd of teenagers moving quickly between lockers and classes.

Having nothing else to do that evening, I invited my friend Maurice to accompany me. A tinge of excitement gripped me as I parked my car in front of a lovely suburban home. Scores of pretty girls and football hunks were milling around. Walking to the large back yard, I found the food and basketball court. After an enjoyable hour of eating and talking, I was ready to leave. But God was about to weave a very important thread into my tapestry of life. At the risk of sounding over Calvinistic, I was predestined to remain.

"Come on inside," someone yelled, and all 100 gregarious teens moved toward the house. Too many bodies and not enough chairs. While sitting on the floor, I surveyed the huge room. The motif was ranch style. In fact, names were even branded into the wooden walls. Up front, a few guys were preparing to create music on a guitar, an accordion, and an inverted bath tub with a stick and a rope attached. All around me sat my peers squashed tightly one against another. My thought had been that we were going to do some dancing. Obviously that wouldn't work because of space limitations. So, what had I gotten myself into?

Moments later, they struck up the "band" and with great gusto the singing commenced. The tunes were totally unfamiliar, but I was well acquainted with the focus of the words. "Jesus" vied for "I" as the predominant word in my vocabulary. However, profanity, not worship, was my mode of usage for this exalted name. It always amazes me how divinity can be consistently dragged down into the gutter by millions. Totally unthinkable would be such a carnal utterance of the name Muhammad. There are even blasphemy laws in certain Muslim countries that prescribe death for any denigration of the person of Muhammad.

But now, in a relevant and attractive context, I was hearing a reverent use of the name Jesus. Next came the testimonies. Accomplished and popular teens stood to their feet and unashamedly testified to a personal, life-changing encounter with Christ. Never in my life had I heard such words.

Ray was a successful salesman for National Cash Register. His home, known to young people as "The Ranch," was the venue for this every Thursday night happening. My first encounter with this handsome, outgoing, middle-aged man followed the songs and testimonies. Casually dressed, Ray stood at the front and held us in rapt attention as, interspersed with memoirs of his days as a bombardier in the Second World War, he simply explained the Gospel. The focus of his message was a constant repetition of the biblical verses, Ephesians 2:8 and 9. He wanted everyone to fully understand that the gift of eternal life is totally free and without condition. By the end of his 45 minute message, it was obvious we would be extremely stupid to refuse such an offer. No cost. No obligation. No commitment. Just accept.

I have come to feel Ray overdid the grace part, indeed coming close to a presentation of "cheap grace." Be that as it may, that evening at the Ranch I was smitten, quietly yet firmly, by the overwhelming mercy of God. Ray closed the meeting by asking all to bow their heads, close their eyes, and signify by a raised hand if they would like to, that very moment, receive eternal salvation in Christ. Meekly, I slipped up my hand. The meeting was soon over.

As the noisy crowd milled about, an extremely pretty girl came over and sat beside me. Within a few moments she had her New Testament open, further explaining the Good News to me. After ten minutes of John, Romans, and Ephesians, she asked if I was ready for the Kingdom. With seventy-five percent attention on the message and twenty-five percent attention on the messenger, I said a one hundred percent "Yes." A simple prayer followed that utterly revolutionized my life.

I was a carnal young man of the world. I was biblically illiterate, not knowing there was an Old and New Testament in the Bible. Peter, John, and Paul were friends at school, but unknown to me as biblical authors. Inerrancy, ecclesiology, and eschatology were as alien to me as algebra. Yet, in the wonderful moment of conversion, my soul took flight on an awesome journey, one without end, yet the destination was and is sure. Who among us can grasp the full meaning and reality of eternity? Why do we Evangelicals react negatively to the phrase, "A leap of faith?" Most assuredly, my conversion from darkness to light and from eternal death to eternal life was not based on cognitive brilliance. Christianity is not labeled as a "knowledge," but rather as a faith. Our belief system is not a 2+2=4 propositional truth. With all my heart I believe in the Word of God. But many of my queries await resolution in that wonderful day to come. For now, I see and know only "as through a glass darkly."

All of the above in no way de-emphasizes the revolutionary effect on my life that was put into motion by my leap of faith. As I left Ray's home that evening, my heart was pounding with excitement. Reaching our little cottage located just behind a bar, I rushed in to give Mom the good news of my conversion. Forcefully and dramatically, I explained God's free gift which I had just accepted. Needless to say, she was overwhelmed by the force of my presentation which ended in an appeal for her to do exactly what I had done an hour earlier. With a rather condescending voice of sarcasm, Mom said, "Phil Jr., you have had an emotional experience. Go to bed and sleep it off. You will have forgotten all about it in the morning."

Lying in bed that night, I read the first three chapters of the Gospel of John which Ray had given me. The Word powerfully impacted me and affirmed my new linkage with Divinity. Who was I, a person of no great heritage or wealth, to be allowed to partake of such a heavenly inheritance? Over the years, whenever doubts and struggles have assailed me, I have many times "returned to my Bethel" and mentally reviewed the events of that Thursday evening.

The next morning I continued my aggressive pursuit of lost souls. Dad and my brother gave the same reaction as Mom, but perhaps a bit less lovingly. In fact, my brother later told me that my father had called the Miami Police Department and asked them to check out this "cult" that his son had attached himself to! It would take a long and frustrating 17 years before any of my family would become believers. I attribute much of that delay to my grossly insensitive initial and ongoing presentation of the Gospel.

In one sense, I had found a new Father and a new community to which I could relate. My earthly father, with whom I had no real affinity, had been exchanged for a heavenly Father. Now I had a Father whom I could respect and be proud of. Without embarrassment, I could introduce Him to all and sundry. It was a good feeling.

As could be expected, I fell madly in love with the beautiful girl who had evangelized me. Fortunately for me, and for her, this led nowhere. But she graciously dropped me with tact. She must have realized my ego and spirituality were both at a fragile state.

Ray's "Ranch" became a second home. In retrospect, I marvel at how Ray and his wife, Sue, could have put up with such a constant flow of young people into their lives. This gracious couple always had time to counsel and interact with their flock. Beach outings and other events contributed to an atmosphere of spirituality that was fun. Not too long after my conversion, Ray was ordained as a Presbyterian minister. His outreach then became a full-time calling with support coming from a number of churches and individuals. He was, by far, the most fruitful personal soul winner that I have ever known.

High school graduation. A very special moment in the life of any teenager. The joy of the occasion was definitely muted by the absence of Mom and Dad. My father never felt comfortable in formal situations. Mom was probably at work. Still, it was an okay night as I spent it in fellowship with my new friends from the Ranch.

Spiritually and academically I was on a fairly good growth curve. The University of Miami was nearby. I took evening classes in their summer school. During the day I worked in a rather mundane job, grinding and painting metal in an ornamental iron shop. My goal was to become a wealthy certified public accountant. The only way for this to be accomplished was by working full time and going to night school.

Things went from bad to worse with Dad. His drinking increased to an intolerable level. Finally, Mom left him, and I followed her into yet another small apartment. Jimmy had already happily married his high school sweetheart. Dad got jolted into reality, swore off drinking, and begged Mom to give him another chance. She capitulated after two months, and they came back together. Amazingly, Dad stayed sober from that point on to his death in his mid-70's. His erratic personality, however, never really changed. Jimmy took over from my grandfather as Dad's financial savior. My brother was unbelievably patient with Dad's demands and idiosyncrasies.

Launching Forth

The summer of 1955 was another major pivotal point in my life. Ray was convinced I showed potential for the ministry. And, to think, I was just four months away from raw heathenism. Controlling sexual urges and refraining from cursing were my front line engagements in spiritual battle. Ministry was a long way from my list of career options. But Ray would not let go. During one session with him that went well past midnight, I finally gave in and agreed to go way up to "Yankee land," to Chattanooga to attend Tennessee Temple College, but only for one year.

As expected, Mom protested, while Dad and my brother were passive. Selling off my Ford was as traumatic as saying good-bye to Mom. The $75 I received from the sale represented my total assets as I boarded the bus for Chattanooga. One could make a case that I was full of presumption… or naïve faith. Anyway, I was ready to give it my best shot.

Divine Threads Within A Human Tapestry

Tennessee Temple was and is a Fundamentalist, independent, Baptist college. Its ethos of conservatism was stretched considerably by the arrival of the "Miami gang" of 15 people. We made an impressive impact. "Why can't we go to movies?" "What, we can't even hold hands?" "No mixed swimming? You've got to be kidding!" Incrementally, we began to merge into the mainstream. Actually, it was not all that bad. Dr. Lee Roberson, the president, was held in highest esteem by all of us students. It was my privilege to be baptized by him. Though certainly not an Ivy League school academically, Temple provided a sincere and godly environment which was just perfect for me as a six month old babe in the Christian faith.

The above notwithstanding, one of my first three roommates (all in the same dorm room) was a homosexual. He seemed to have an effeminate manner, but he never made any sexual move toward me. One day I walked into the room and found he had packed up and left. Someone had caught him and another student in a compromising act. Both were immediately expelled.

A few years later I traveled one summer with a student Gospel team. Bob, the leader, was highly esteemed at Temple. Early in the summer our team was staying at a home where, because of inadequate space, Bob and I shared a double bed. Around 2 AM I awoke as I felt Bob's hand slowly making its way up my thigh. Immediately, I threw his hand away from my body. No words were exchanged. My emotions were taut as many questions tumbled through my mind. Was Bob a *Homo*?" What was he doing leading a Gospel team? Was there something about me that made him think I would respond to his overtures? I was ready to leave.

The next morning I related my story to a godly team member who, in turn, talked to Bob. No denial of the act was made, but Bob, for the first time, admitted he was a divorcee. Therefore, he excused his move as that which was done in his sleep and had been natural in his married state. No further problem occurred that summer. Bob's lie was revealed years later when he approached some straight young men for sex. They beat him severely.

I have always had a strong aversion toward homosexuals. Their sex act seems totally unnatural and dirty. Perhaps this is why the

Lord has put a number of non-practicing homosexual-oriented young men in my path. They have, in tears, shared the hurt and pain they experience as they struggle for sexual purity. Many of them are bisexual, which means they are being attacked on two fronts. Perplexity reigns in their hearts as they try to figure out why God has allowed them to be tested so severely. Their bodies cry out for sexual expression while their spirits long for victorious release from temptation. My empathy for "Christian homosexuals" has risen to a high level. I do not condone that which the Bible clearly condemns. But my heart goes out to those caught up in drives and urges that, they say, are not their choice or desire. They need our care and help in order to change, not just our censure. Battle on, brave soldiers. May our Lord grant victory and peace in the midst of a struggle that most of us cannot begin to comprehend.

A "watershed" event occurred during my first few months at Temple. My first job involved hitchhiking five miles to and from an A&P grocery store where I was employed as a cashier. One day a black man came through my check-out stand with several six packs of beer. With a smile on my face, I chided him for purchasing a product which was not in his best interests. He took no offense.

The lady cashier next to me overheard the conversation and reported me to the manager, who became extremely angry and told me there could never be a repeat of such an incident. If it was against my convictions to sell alcohol, then I could quit. I told him I would think about it.

That night I was overcome with perplexity. My school bills were barely being met by the income from my job. In fact, at that time, I was not even spending money on a Coke or candy bar. There was no other job in view. Should I launch out by faith or smother my personal convictions and keep on selling beer?

At the ripe old age of nine months in the Lord, I decided I must quit. To stand for my convictions was priority. It would be up to the Lord to take care of any problems that might arise from such a decision.

Within a few days of leaving A&P another cashier position was found where alcohol was not sold. I made more money and was able to keep the job right through college. This was one of the early lessons I received in the importance of launching out in faith in order to maintain fidelity to my Lord.

My four years as a Bible major at Temple were exhausting. Attending three summer schools allowed me to take a reduced load during the year. My work averaged over 30 hours a week, plus travel. Besides this, I supervised an evangelistic outreach to Black children each Sunday. Then there was always time for dating, which usually meant taking a girl to church or sitting on a bench together for a few minutes at 9:30 PM after I returned from work. Study took place late at night. My ironclad, long-term commitment to one hour of daily devotions took place while at Temple. This was usually performed at 5 AM in an empty classroom across from my dorm. Some have declared my ritual to be legalism. I prefer to consider it a necessary discipline for spiritual survival.

There was little contact between my family and me those four years. They definitely considered me some kind of religious fanatic. This view was reinforced by my occasional evangelistic-type letter to Mom and Dad, usually sent right after a guest speaker at Temple exhorted the students to write such notes. I did long for my family to become Christians. Years of fervent prayer were directed to this end. As far as I can recall, neither my parents or brother ever gave one cent to me during this period. This included the absence of Christmas and birthday presents. This void was keenly felt, particularly as it related to Mom. At 17 years old, I had embarked on a lonely journey, cut off from family and financial backing. Sink or swim. I had permanently pushed off from home port into the deep, and at times turbulent, sea of life.

Missions

Temple's annual missionary conference was powerful. My emotions were stirred as I heard the story of the martyrdom of Jim Elliot. And how challenging it was to learn of attempts to reach the stone-age natives of Irian Jaya. Islam was presented as an almost impregnable barrier to the Gospel. Missionaries would tell of a lifetime of service among Muslims with only negligible results. Yet, God loved Muslims. There were no exclusions. Gradually the Holy Spirit weaned me from my personal desire for wealth and security, and in 1958 I made my covenant with the Lord for missionary service. I had been a Christian for three years.

As I looked at the lost world statistically, it became evident Islam and Communism were the neglected ideologies that needed Christ. At that time only Muslim countries were open to missionary presence. My heart moved in that direction. A fellow student from Pakistan pressed upon me the need for Christian witness in his country which was 97 percent Muslim. It was not too long before he had a recruit. At last, I had found a cause big enough to live for and, if necessary, to die for.

Senioritis is how the wags might describe it. Symptoms are: a state of mild mental confusion, physical restlessness, and emotional dissonance. Cause? Reaching the exalted status of college senior without being engaged. Well, I wasn't in a state of total panic, but I was wondering why none of the girls I had been dating seemed to "connect." I had never been engaged or even close to it. The idea of becoming a single male missionary to Pakistan for the rest of my life didn't excite me. But I was not about to make the wrong choice. My standard for a life partner was extremely high.

For some time I had noticed an attractive sophomore who always seemed to have a boyfriend, including at one time the president of the student body. She was possessed of a quiet grace that was winsome. The only negatives were that she had short hair and ever-present suitors. Oh, yes, I didn't like her name, Julia. So, I kept my eye on her, waiting for an interval between guys. I figured I could persuade her to let her hair grow out and surely she would not mind if I called her Julie, a name with a pleasant resonance.

Finally, my day of opportunity arrived. The first big date occurred in January of 1959. I was quickly stricken; even worse than I was with my first "love" back in the tenth grade. This time I knew the stakes were high, really high. From all indications she was reciprocally interested. Romance blossomed.

We possess a special 8 x 10 inch black and white picture of us taken during this time on Lookout Mountain, a mile above Chattanooga. I am trim with dark hair. Julie (a first name happily agreed upon), sitting close by on a large rock, has hair no longer to be described as short.

What particularly attracted me toward Julie was her peaceful composure. Her phlegmatic temperament accepted life with a measure of stoicism that I could only dream of. My mood swings were quite mercurial. Highs were emotive and exhilarating. Lows were melancholic and depressing. If ever I was to survive, I would need a spouse of opposite personality who would have the capacity to calm the troubled waters. There was a sense of awe that such a gentle spirited person could be attracted to someone who tended to be somewhat bombastic and moody. That awe continues to this day.

We began to date with serious intent.

In late June of 1959, while in summer school, I was suddenly and inexplicably stricken with a high level of nervous tension. I had no idea what was going on. Tension permeated every nerve ending in my body. Could I, as a 21 year old, be experiencing a nervous breakdown? Surely not, because I was told such problems were the domain of the non-believer or the carnal Christian. No huge hidden sin controlled my life. With all my heart I desired to follow my Lord. So what was completely overwhelming me?

I had no appetite, so I began to lose serious weight. Feeling rotten, I checked into the school infirmary where I remained a number of days. A nervous disorder was said to indicate a lack of trust in Jesus, therefore I was hesitant to tell the school nurse or anyone else how I really felt. The exception was when I went to a doctor. He seemed to understand what was going on and prescribed what was probably a mild tranquilizer. This was unacceptable to me, so I dumped them after a few days.

Trying desperately to figure it all out, I increased my devotional time. My next move was to break up with Julie. Perhaps the Lord was displeased with our relationship. This put Julie into a spin. But nothing I did seemed to help, with the exception of drinking lots of tea or Coke. The caffeine had a soothing effect on my nervous system.

This condition continued, with lesser or greater intensity, for 14 long years. Apart from Julie and a doctor or two, no one ever knew what I was experiencing. The "attacks" of tension were without warning. Any time and anywhere, I would seize up. The worst times would be when I was speaking in a church. I would cover my emotions and tough it out.

So what really was the cause of this obvious overload of my nervous system? A few guesses would be:

- Hereditary influence from my grandfather's breakdown.

- The rejection I experienced from my peers during my obese years.

- Conflict with a dad whom I could not love or respect.

- The accumulated effect of scores of moves around South Florida.

- Lack of family support in my Christian life.

- Excessive work and study for four years.

- Anxiety concerning a decision about marriage in particular and the future in general.

- A strong stream of melancholy in my temperament.

Most likely it was some combination of all of the above.

One strong character trait emerged out of those dark years. Tenacity and perseverance have been burned deeply into my soul. How easy it would have been to call it quits along the way. But the Lord just kept reinforcing me and giving strength to press on even when I barely could place one foot in front of the other. The down side of all this, I guess, is my impatience with those who so quickly disengage and leave the battle.

In confusion, I started dating Julie again, but with some reservation. I wanted her to have a stronger personal call to missions. Also, I wondered, with my struggles, would it be fair to tie her down to a guy with a future that was fraught with uncertainty. I knew where I wanted to go, but I was not at all sure I had the resources to get there. The threads of the tapestry were seemingly wandering off from the design.

At the end of a terrible summer, I walked the aisle to be the first of our Parshall clan that I know of to receive a B.A. degree. As expected, there was no family member present to join in the celebration. Even with all of the emotional pain I was experiencing, it was good to have "finished the course." I was now ready for the next chapter of life.

Chapter 4

Further Preparation

Prior to graduation from Temple, I had concluded that I needed further training in missions. Moody Bible Institute in Chicago was highly recommended as a school which could meet my needs through their one year post graduate program. Putting Julie "on hold," I left for the Windy City.

Though I had an amiable roommate, I was lonely at Moody. Being four years senior to most of the students, I did not fit into the social patterns of my dorm. The girls did not seem to attract me. Thus, I endured my longest stretch without dating. Julie was still in mind. I was not ready to drop her, neither was I prepared to commit. The gray zone was rather miserable for both of us.

After a few months at Moody two powerful influences began to close in on my life. First was disillusionment with my spiritual growth. Tennessee Temple's emphasis that sanctification is gradual, based on one's commitment to prayer, Bible study, witnessing, and obedience sounded logical. But, try as I might, I still felt as though life was a treadmill not allowing for forward movement.

Any number of professors at Moody had been influenced by the British-based Keswick movement. They spoke often of the possibility of living on a higher spiritual plane, one that did not lock a person into a repetitious syndrome of sin—conviction—confession—forgiveness—then sin and back through the cycle. The believer, it was stated, should develop a deep hunger and thirst for the reality of the indwelling Christ. This would be followed by a soul-searching confession of sin. Finally, the seeker would abdicate self in favor of the "exchanged life" of "not I, but Christ." This process would lead one to enter into the rest spoken of in Hebrews 4.

Definitely this formula for a higher attainment of spirituality communicated to my barren soul. How I thirsted for the streams of living water to flow freshly throughout my being. No longer was I willing to remain bogged down in a Romans 7 experience of fleshly defeat. This hunger for God became almost obsessive. Books were read, Keswick leaders consulted, passionate prayer made, all with the goal of becoming more intimate with my Lord and Savior. After all, I was promised in Scripture that I would be filled if I hungered and thirsted for righteousness. And being of choleric temperament, I wanted it right NOW!

It would, however, take time. Several months, in fact. The Lord desired to enlarge the boundaries of the tapestry, but only with His design of depth and permanence. This was to be no shallow work by the Master Designer.

On the second floor of my dorm was an unobtrusive room with several chairs, a bare floor, and a single light bulb. Quite an unpretentious setting for a life-changing encounter with an awesome God. But late one afternoon, I entered this empty Prayer Room and began to cry aloud to the Lord for the "higher-plane experience." Oh, how my thirst for God had crescendoed to the point of utter desperation! "Now, Lord, yes, now, send down your refreshing balm for my weary soul. Fill this empty vessel with the reality of your indwelling presence. Lift me to the heavenlies so that I may know release from this debilitating yoke of bondage to sin that so constantly besets me."

The next moments defy description and analysis. It was as if the heavens of brass suddenly and inexplicably were cataclysmically torn apart. God was revealed in all His terror and power and love. I stood before him naked and undone. And then it was as if I was tenderly reclothed in new garments... clean, soft, sweet-smelling, all-embracing garments. I was being enfolded into a mystical oneness with the indwelling Christ.

My heart leaped for joy, somewhat like the newborn lamb that has just been released from the stygian darkness of the womb. Every taut nerve ending shut down, allowing God's incomprehensible peace to flow ever so freely throughout every crevice of my body.

No shouting. No speaking ecstatic utterances. Just peace, wonderful, wonderful peace. The Hound of Heaven had pursued; the hunted one had surrendered; and the resulting encounter was a foretaste of the glory to be experienced more fully at the Marriage Supper of the Lamb in Heaven. How sweet it was.

Having a personal philosophy that says, "What works for me will work for you," led me to share rather forcefully (somewhat like my conversion experience... will I ever learn?) with all and sundry the wonders and glories of my encounter with the Lord. Fortunately, I was within the acceptable theological framework of Moody. Friends were warmly open to my exhortations for them to seek to duplicate my experience, though few, if any, probably actually did.

The next four months were ethereal. Christ was so real, sin so unappealing. Prayer was a delight. Biblical truths ignited within my innermost being. My nervous tension went into remission. How could Christianity possibly get better?

During this time I made a brief trip back to Temple. There I set forth my experience as a norm for all the more "legalistic" Christians at my alma mater. I urged Julie to commence her spiritual journey in exactly the way I had done. How unfair it was (as I have learned later) to lay this burden on a person of phlegmatic temperament. How uniquely the Holy Spirit moves in each of His children. I was still unsure of my future with Julie. As I joyfully returned to Moody in my enhanced spiritual state, I left behind a confused and bewildered young lady.

Incrementally, the flaming fire began to lose its intensity. Soon what remained was the soft glow of red embers. The emotional highs leveled off, but the reality lingered on, even to this day.

Lessons learned: (1) How important it is to have a vital, intimate, ongoing relationship with Christ. (2) God's dealings with His children are tailor made. I have no right to prescribe a formula, but it's okay to make discreet suggestions. (3) Spiritual highs involve the instability of our emotions. Without doubt there will be valleys to be endured as well as mountain peaks to be enjoyed. (4) Perseverance throughout the Christian's life is the greatest test of anyone's personal spiritual experience. I have little patience with this or that prescribed formula which causes the hungry soul to flare upward, and soon leaves nothing but scorched earth. Better steady and lasting than spectacular and temporary.

To be utterly honest, though I am a very emotional person, I fear emotion. No, spiritual exuberance does not parallel with the rightness of unbridled enthusiasm at a football game as some of my friends have suggested. That is an inadequate analogy. We, in Christianity, are dealing with the very core being of self. As we confront our Maker in worship and surrender, we must constantly evaluate ourselves.

Is emotion manipulated to achieve an "atmosphere?" Do we favor the ecstatic moments for how good they make us feel? In a highly charged religious service, are our baser sexual drives likewise stimulated? Are we more vulnerable to fleshly pressures within an emotionally volatile setting? Can the heavenly highs be sustained or do we come back to earth with a resounding and depressing thud?

Now, to surprise the reader. Some of my most esteemed friends are mainline Pentecostals and enthusiastic Charismatics. My spiritual guru for several decades was the late Calvin Olsen, an Assemblies of God missionary who spent over 30 years serving the Lord in Bangladesh. Ron Peck, the director for Muslim ministries of the Assemblies of God, is another close friend. These are the reputable believers who are aware of the dangers of ever using emotion as a tool for anything except as a facilitator in our worship of Christ. To them I owe much.

The opposite extreme is, likewise, a dangerous route. It involves overly cognitive dead orthodoxy. Emotional expression is prohibited to the extent that a raised hand during worship would invite a scornful visit by a deacon during the following week. Overall, I see this side of the continuum as a greater repugnance to God. Certainly the Old Testament is full of worship patterns that are joyful and exuberant.

So, with all the above explanations and qualifiers, I am indeed grateful for that moment in Norton Hall when I powerfully encountered the living Christ. I have grave doubts if I would have persevered to this point in my ministry without that life-changing experience.

Operation Mobilization

The other milestone event which occurred at Moody commenced when I began to hear about a radical student who was making big-time waves among the undergrads. GEORGE VERWER. To those who know him or Operation Mobilization (OM), the organization which he founded, few further words are necessary.

George, in 1959-60, was a revolutionary senior who had for two years been the talk of the Moody campus. Short, thin, and with a rather large nose, George was no lady killer. Rather, his empowerment obviously was God-related. His message was that of radical discipleship, "Forsake all. Just keep enough possessions and money to enable you to live frugally. Give up chocolate bars and Cokes. Move out in missions. Burn your bridges behind you."

Unforgettable… the first time I heard George speak. The occasion was an all-night prayer meeting in one of the classrooms. Somewhere around midnight as this human dynamo was at full steam, he blurted out, "You young people must get off your butts and move out for God." The rest of the night was a blur. I was in shock. Was this appropriate language for a student leader? What a guy!

Soon I was hooked. The love and fire burning in the souls of those zealots had deeply affected me. Within days I joined the "pilgrimage" to George's dorm room where I deposited a few boxes of my college textbooks. We OMers, in the biblical tradition of forsaking all, were ridding ourselves of the extraneous. George, in turn, sold those books given by the enlightened to those who were as yet unenlightened. All proceeds went to missions.

In one sense, I found George to be a bit uncouth. He was so compulsive, radical, and denunciatory. George had the zeal, but what about the fruits of the Spirit—love, peace, gentleness, and patience? One incident helped me put this budding man of God into perspective.

45

Over 100 students were sitting in a class, listening to a highly respected senior professor lecture on the spiritual dynamics required of those desiring to be missionaries. In a calm, gracious manner, he spoke of some Moody students who were being extremely critical of faculty and administration. He humbly warned us students of the dangers of sweeping denunciations of the status quo.

When he finished, from the back of the room, George Verwer rose to his feet and humbly confessed to his verbal sins committed the day before. He further stated that he had slackened off on his personal devotional time and requested prayer that he might be more fully dedicated to the Lord.

After he sat down, the professor explained that he was not just referring to George. If he had been, he would have talked to him personally. The problem, however, was more widespread. All was done in a beautiful spirit of humility and grace. It was then I realized George had a sensitive component within his temperament, not one always perceived when listening to his rather bombastic pulpit presentations.

Friends were amazed how I could spend so much time in OM activities, be the leader of the Muslim Prayer Band, and also work a part-time job with Moody Press. The simple answer was that I had reduced my second semester academic load to an absolute minimum. My newfound focus in life was to know Christ and to make Him known.

Mexico

That summer of 1960 found me in the back of a dilapidated van making my way from Chicago to Veracruz, Mexico. Ralph, an African-American OM "insider," was the designated leader of our team of three, the third young evangelizer being Jerry, a gentle soul.

Soon after crossing the Mexican border, our vehicle was stopped for a customs check. Ralph became extremely agitated as the officials looked over our many packets of evangelistic literature. Becoming suspicious, they decided to start a smuggling case against Ralph. Off he went to a filthy prison. The van was confiscated, leaving Jerry and me bewildered, penniless, and more than a bit upset with Ralph for his display of fearful panic. In a moment of time, the "romance" of being God's mighty instruments for world evangelization had dissipated like a puff of smoke on a windy day.

After making an SOS collect call to OM in Chicago, Jerry and I, around 10 PM, started wandering around the small, sleepy Mexican border town, trying to find a bench to sleep on. As soon as we got settled down, we would see a policeman making his way toward us. So, off we would go. And so it went for most of that memorable night. Finally, we ended up sleeping for a few hours in someone's front yard.

A few days later help did arrive. A lawyer was hired who most likely negotiated a bribe with the judge. Upon release, Ralph was found to have metamorphosed from a gutsy choleric into a paranoid recluse. Indications were that we were in for a long difficult summer.

Veracruz is a friendly seacoast town in southeast Mexico. Our team of three was billeted in a Sunday school room of a Pentecostal church. We could barely say hello, good-bye, or count to ten in Spanish. Sales were minimal, food was uninteresting, the climate was like unto Purgatory and sliding downward, team fellowship with Ralph was strained, and worst of all, our evangelistic zeal was quickly receding into oblivion. So this was missionary life!

Around mid-summer, Julie began receiving increasingly frequent and increasingly romantic letters from points southward. If my life was going to be spent in Purgatory, it would not be a solitary confinement. No way! Miraculously, Julie had decided to put her dating life on hold until I received some specific direction for my life. She quickly responded affirmatively to my invitation to visit me in Miami at the end of the summer. Now, my only problem was how to get to Miami.

OM offered to give me a lift up to Texas. They suggested that then I could hitchhike over to South Florida. Somehow that idea didn't thrill me. So I wrote to a benefactor explaining my need, thinly disguised as a prayer request. By return mail I received a money order that would cover my airfare and a very cheap hotel fare for an overnight enroute.

It was with no great regret I bid my teammates and Veracruz *adios*. Flying into another Mexican city, I asked the stewardess where I could find inexpensive accommodation for the night. She offered to share her hotel room with me. After a tough summer, I am grateful I had enough residual spirituality to turn down her proposition.

In retrospect, and with some degree of objectivity, I can see my Mexico experience as a microcosm of that which was to come in my future missionary career. Packed into the 2½ months was tension, heat, discouragement, temptation, and failure. Yet, character was being formed within the crucible of fiery testings. I had confirmed that OM was not to be my mission board of choice, but at the same time, my gratitude and admiration for that organization commenced that summer and has grown immeasurably over the years. George Verwer is at the top of my list of missionary statesmen. He is a devout zealot. George has held on tenaciously to what can only be termed revolutionary Christianity. Both in his personal life and in his ministry he has sought to model total Christian commitment. The long haul perspective has judged him worthy of honor. Today, OM is one of the largest mission organizations in the world. It has been God's instrument to influence hundreds of thousands of lives for the Kingdom.

Julie

My return to Miami and to family was a bit tense, but the prospect of Julie's upcoming visit made life more exciting. And what a visit it was! One evening we drove in Dad's car to a small island which jutted out from the causeway that connects Miami and Miami Beach. As we sat looking at the thousands of glittering lights of two of this planet's most gorgeous cities, I proceeded to make an analytical, tentative "proposal." My absolute poverty and ongoing emotional stress were described. Other inadequacies of my life were included in my presentation. I ended up by saying if all went well in the next year, I wanted Julie to marry me; and, oh, yes, I told her I was madly in love with her! To some, all this may sound a bit overly cognitive, but these past decades have affirmed my *modus operandi.*

Julie's gracious response was an unqualified "Yes." Little did she know what an awesome journey she had embarked upon with the articulation of that one small word. I assured her my love was stronger than diamonds, therefore I would forego giving her an engagement ring! Also, we agreed to exchange simple wedding bands ordered from a discount catalog. To this day outward symbols have meant little to us. We usually only exchange cards on birthdays, at Christmas, and on our anniversary. But my discount wedding ring is in a special category. It strongly affirms my absolute commitment to my lover until death do us part. The ring has never left my finger from our moment of union.

Julie returned to Tennessee Temple for her senior year. Some months earlier I had decided to join Missionary Internship's seven month program in Detroit, Michigan. In the Lord's wonderful providence, I was placed as an intern in the well know and highly respected Highland Park Baptist Church. Working with teenagers was a delight. This ministry also gave me an opportunity to meet the parents who were the pillars of the large church. A love affair commenced which remains until this day. In a sense, I was an orphan without a home church. Highland Park adopted me (and, after our marriage, Julie) as their very own and added us to their missions budget. We are tremendously grateful to this outstanding church for their consistent expressions of love and significant support.

On Mondays the interns met together for a time of training under the leadership of Fred Renich. It was then, way back in 1960, that Fred introduced me to the temperament studies. This categorization of personality types has helped me to better understand myself and others. Interestingly, I conclude I am a combination of all of the temperaments except phlegmatic and that Julie is almost pure phlegmatic. And it has been a great merger.

In late May, 1961, I journeyed back to Tennessee Temple to see my fiancée graduate. She had been voted the "Most Typical" student of her graduating class. A week later, in her small hometown of La Rue, Ohio, we took a pledge of commitment that mysteriously and wonderfully brought our two bodies into a union of one. Over eighty young people and their parents from Highland Park drove several hours south from Detroit to join in our wedding celebration. With a borrowed car, we took off for a brief honeymoon to a friend's cottage in Northern Michigan. We truly had stepped out in faith.

Immediately following our honeymoon we attended the candidate school of Ceylon and India General Mission. In 1967, CIGM changed its name to International Christian Fellowship and, in 1989, merged with SIM International. My ministerial journey has been with one mission but it has had three different names during my tenure.

Deputation was a hassle. We added up our wedding gift money and had $700 to buy an old Ford for transportation. I had few contacts and even less money. We were committed to full-time support raising, so there were times of wondering from where our next meal would come. Tension increased to the point that I was not at all sure I could endure the upcoming hassles of East Pakistan. If I was not able to run with the footmen, how would I make it with the horses?

In desperation, I invited a Christian surgeon friend to our little apartment. When he arrived at 11 PM, I unloaded all of my struggles of nervous tension and subsequent doubts on him. This was a pivotal moment in my life. He could have easily flashed a red signal that potentially would have ended my missionary aspirations. I tend to feel, if I had been in his place, that is what I would have done. Instead, Howard spoke words of faith and settled assurance, that, with the strength of the Lord, I would be able to go forth and fulfill my calling as a missionary to the Muslim world. He did suggest I try gardening, table games, and exercise as recreational and emotional therapy while on the field. Unfortunately the above hold no interest for me, and that would include the whole range of the sports world. I do, however, enjoy reading and travel, both areas conveniently fitting into my professional involvements.

Our leaving of parents was harder for Julie than for me. She came from a close knit, supportive family. But I must admit to ambivalence concerning many of Julie's network of loved ones. On one hand, they provided tremendous stability for her as a person and as a Christian. Spending years on a small farm helped prepare her for the rigors of East Pakistan village life. On the other hand, I basically failed in my role as a son-in-law. I am a city guy who just could not seem to relate to a rural Ohio lifestyle. The farmers spoke in a countrified slang I couldn't appreciate. Their concern for crops, weather, and gossip was thoroughly mundane to me.

Julie is a clone of her dad, easy going and patient. But I did clash with her Mom, who possessed a temperament much too similar to mine. However, we did do better in the years preceding their deaths. I will be forever grateful for the Oberdier blood that courses through my wife's veins as well as for the laid back community that so helped form Julie's beautiful personality.

Miraculously, our support was pledged in a brief eight months. In March of 1962, Julie, at age 22, and I with my 24 years of youth, boarded a freighter in New York with great aspirations and even greater fears. We, at last, were on our way to one of the least evangelized countries in the world.

Chapter 5

On To The Battle

Twenty-six days on a slow moving ship is not really my style. There were nine of us passengers: Two nuns, a reprobate Indian Hindu who ate beef, a worldly young American lady who delighted to flirt with the ship's officers, and Chuck and Joanna Foster with their nine-month-old daughter Julie Ann who, like us, were CIGM missionaries going to East Pakistan. We were able to break the monotony with a few brief port visits, the most interesting one being Port Said in Egypt. In the middle of the night the town was totally alive, catering to the desires of the hundreds of passengers who had disembarked from another ship which had just berthed nearby. Without a doubt, the journey through the Suez Canal was the highlight of the trip. The canal was unbelievably narrow. All of the events that have occurred in that area since 1962 have taken on a visual reality because of our cruise down the Suez.

And then, on the 26th day, the distant lights of Karachi, Pakistan, came into view. Within a few hours we were met in the port and taxied to an Anglican guest house which was located in the heart of that huge, bustling city. So many new sights, smells, and sounds, all overwhelmingly bombarding the senses. After a sleepless night (our first under a mosquito net), we boarded a prop plane for our slow flight over to Dhaka, East Pakistan.

Was it fate, God's will, or poor planning that we walked out of our plane into the 100 degree blast of heat that signaled the onset of the two hottest months in the country's calendar? Though I am from

Florida, I still had never encountered such debilitating, humid heat. Met by our CIGM missionaries, we were soon on our way to a "hotel." That was quite a superlative for a run down structure alongside a railroad track. I ended up sharing my bedroll with friendly cockroaches on the floor between Chuck Foster and our field leader, separated by a grimy wall from my beloved bride of nine months. She was with the other lady missionaries. Our first night apart!

The next day three-wheeled motorized *monsters* known as "baby taxis" and driven by speed addicts who delighted to miss other vehicles by millimeters while driving at 35 mph, took us four miles to the river steamer terminal which was located among the masses in Old Dhaka. It was a journey to be taken many times in the future, but never one like unto the first. Mary Macdonald, from England, was our middle-aged station supervisor. She was a zealous worker, totally committed to a simple lifestyle. This commitment revealed itself in her choice of tickets. We found ourselves laying out our bedrolls on the open deck of the steamer, surrounded by at least 50 sets of staring, inquisitive brown eyes. Arranging the cane furniture we had just purchased in a circle around us, we settled down for the night.

After a fitful eight hours of on and off sleep, I awoke to find myself amazingly sound of body and sane of mind. Around 6 AM our steamer nudged its bow against the dock. Immediately scores of coolies jumped on and, speaking in an unknown tongue, converged on our little settlement. Mary, a master at "haggling," spent ten minutes seeking to minimize their pay for our courier services. This struck me as miserly. However, it did not take me long to join into the cultural mainstream and become part of the system, though I never learned to enjoy it.

Manikganj

Our ragtag line of coolies and missionaries began the single file, one mile trek into the sleepy little village of Manikganj. Dogs barked, children taunted, and adults gaped. Soon we were making our way down an alley to Mary's house, the domicile of the first-ever female missionary in that town since creation. I hold the honor of being the first white man to have lived there. Understandably, this created a perpetual circus effect for the town dwellers, with us in the middle ring as the main attraction.

Mary's rented home was a small tin dwelling. It was a perfect retainer for heat. This was to be our abode for one month while we waited for our shipment to arrive. Certainly Mary sought to make us comfortable, but culture shock was attacking on all fronts. The food was a taste-neutralizing spicy hot; the weather well-illustrated Dante's writings; the dust was all-permeating; and our hard bed consisted of a thin cotton mattress laid over a wooden frame criss-crossed with rope netting.

After a few days of what appeared to be premeditated delay, Mary finally walked us the half mile to our own new home. Perhaps Mary had been a bit hyperbolous when she wrote to us in the States saying she had been able to rent us the nicest house in Manikganj. The main two rooms were all tin except the front wall and two tiny closet-like rooms. Across a small courtyard in the back were another two small cement rooms separated by a toilet which consisted of two bricks on either side of a small hole which emptied into a septic tank. Over the next years we developed good leg muscles from prolonged squatting.

When we were alone again, Julie cried. God has given many women a wonderful emotional response to life's turbulent moments. I have always marveled at how much better Julie feels immediately following a short but fervent crying session. This was one of those historical moments which called for just such a response.

Could this tin shack ever metamorphose into a home? As only a farm girl can do, Julie went to work on that place with zeal and determination. After we cleared our five 55 gallon drums and two crates of personal effects from the port customs office, my wife was able to create a cozy refuge from the storms of life.

Particularly difficult was the "holey" tin. These openings were in our bedroom wall that bordered a Muslim family's compound. As we lay on our bed we could look toward that wall and often see six or eight kids' eyes checking out the foreigners' activities. We tried plastering the holes with pages from TIME magazine, but soon there would be a finger pushing through the inadequate obstruction.

Oh, the joys of living five years without a watt of electricity! Our Coleman pressure lantern did an acceptable job producing the probable equivalent of a 40 watt light bulb. I would love to meet and thank the creative person who dreamed up the idea of a kerosene fan. It had a burner underneath which, after the blade was spun, would crank pistons into action and, amazingly, produce circulating air. The only problem was the smoke from the burner which proceeded up a small smokestack and into the room. We had two of these medieval miracles. On the really hot nights I would position them both very near our bed, get drenched with water, pile in, and try my best to get to sleep before I dried off.

Also in our household inventory of relative affluence was a three foot high kerosene refrigerator. I spent the whole term trying to figure out on a scale of 1 to 10 whether it was a 6 or a 4. If the latter, I should have thrown it in the pond behind our house. Apart from it not being really cold, was the problem created by our only being able to purchase dirty and watered down kerosene. As a Christian, I am quite incapable of describing the depths of frustration I felt as, scores of times, I would wake up between 2 and 3 AM to the strong smell of putrid smoke. Mechanically, I would arise, pull out the heavy tank, clean the wick, relight it, and reinsert it in place. One of the few levels of sanctification I have reached in my life was demonstrated by the fact that I never turned to my wife in bed and groggily said, "Your turn."

An open well in our front yard provided our water, which was first strained and then boiled for drinking. I supervised the construction of a "bush shower." A shower head was soldered into the bottom of a five gallon bucket. This would then be filled with water and lifted six feet up in the air by rope and pulley. It was positioned in one side of the kitchen area. The only near tragedy occurred one day when the full container came crashing to the floor as a frayed section of the rope gave way. I had, seconds before, moved to one side to reach for a bar of soap.

After some months we were able to give rent advances and persuade our landlord to tear down the tin walls and replace them with bricks as well as to build two additional rooms onto the main structure, so we could be totally under one roof. This was done because erosion had caused the back rooms to give way and tumble into the pond. Our tin roof, which so effectively radiated heat downward, remained with us to the end.

Floods inundated the town each year with varying intensity. I well recall the year when water lapped at our top step. The local boatman took me from our house to any point in the village I wanted to go.

The market displayed a variety of foods on a seasonal basis. During the four mild winter months (November to February) we greatly enjoyed a fair selection of vegetables, especially tomatoes. The rest of the year was slim pickings. Fish and emaciated goat were available daily. Beef was to be found on the average once every ten days. A real treat! Chickens were not worth buying. I never got used to the strong duck eggs, which were our only option.

Julie is a fantastic cook... *now*. Then, it was a process, one which caused me to lose 20 pounds our first weeks in the country. She was gradually able to learn how to make the most delicious curries. Some years later, Julie compiled a cook book which also contained hints for foreigners to survive in the country. It became a best seller and was even marketed in posh hotels in Dhaka.

Language study for me was a Mt. Everest-sized challenge. Bengali is difficult in every area, including its most unique script. While at Moody, I took a course in phonetics and made my lowest grade ever in my academic pilgrimage. In desperation I asked the professor if I would be able to learn a foreign language. With supernatural faith she replied that I could, but it would take tremendous effort and determined application. Okay, so be it. On to the battle.

For 2¾ years, five days a week, the wind-up alarm clock would spew forth a most irritating shrill sound at 4:30 AM. It was time to arise, have devotions, eat breakfast, and then at 6:30 have my language lesson. Our Hindu teacher was perhaps the most patient, gracious person I have ever met. Never did a look of despair course over his face as he heard my aspirated sounds gushing forth like a hurricane instead of a subdued, gentle whiff of breath.

Julie, with a natural aptitude for languages, invested two hours a day in study while I fervently labored an average of nine hours. The first year and a half we were full time in language study. This was reduced to half time the second year. The interesting point is, combining the cumulative grades for the two major exams, we came out with exactly the same score. That notwithstanding, Julie is much better in Bengali than I am. Even now, every unusual sounding word presents a formidable challenge to me. But I did prove the worth of perseverance those early years in East Pakistan.

Within a year of our initial arrival in the country, Mary Macdonald had turned over the small Bible Correspondence School to us for oversight. We were able to secure an all tin office just in front of our home. The number of students grew rapidly. Also several other missions began cooperating with us. This was a fulfilling ministry conducted in tandem with language study. We hired a national Christian to assist us in the clerical work.

Bengalis

Without a doubt the foremost hassle during our Manikganj pilgrimage related to undisciplined Bengali kids. Permissive parents allowed the children a free rein; that is until their patience was exhausted. At that time they would become excessively abusive and usually throw the child violently on the ground. There were exceptions, but this was common behavior. And so the kids felt quite free to hassle the foreigners without fear of parental retribution.

Some of my most intense moments of nervous tension occurred as small urchins threw rocks on our tin roof and then scampered away to anonymity in the late night darkness. Another favorite "fun thing" was to bang on our gate with all the strength eight-year-olds could muster and then run away. The last category of irritation related to young, cheeky students calling us names like "Red Monkey" as we walked down the street. To one degree or another, all foreigners in the past and up to the present have had to endure such taunts.

In all of my travels I have never been among a people with such an innate, compelling sense of curiosity. We few white-skinned people among the millions of brown complexioned Bengalis made a perfect target for this genetic trait. While waiting for a boat, bus, or train, we could always count on a dozen gaping adults forming a circle around us, watching our every muscle twitch. Deep conversations of analysis would take place, particularly if they were unaware that we were understanding their profound speculations. Young lady missionaries found this behavior most offensive, as did we young husbands while accompanying our wives in public. Nothing we said to them seemed to daunt their curiosity.

Having thus unburdened my soul of the negative relational conflicts experienced for twenty years, let me hasten to add the positive features of the Bengali people. Interestingly, at the top of the list is their family life. To be sure, wife-beating does take place, but even with Quranic permission to "scourge" one's rebellious spouse, I find such unacceptable behavior probably to be no more common than that reported in the United States. The divorce rate hovers above 40 percent in the Western world. My empirical estimate for divorce and desertion in Bangladesh would be placed at no more than 20 percent. Though Muslims are allowed to have up to four wives, the norm throughout their community is only one.

We have been privileged to have an intimate relationship with Muslim Bengali families. Julie and I have been able to penetrate the usually closed doors, the inner rooms of homes where real family life takes place. This is particularly true of Dr. Ali (about whom more will be said later) and his extended clan. The love dynamics I observed in this pious Muslim family would compare favorably with any evangelical Christian counterpart I have ever encountered.

Young people do at times seriously rebel against parental authority, but such acts are considered a great shame on the family. The preservation of family honor is of utmost importance. "Son of," followed by the father's name is often written after the son's name. The father's shame or honor is part and parcel of the son's identity. This integration serves as an effective deterrent to many social problems.

The Bengalis reach out in love and sacrifice to one and all within the extended blood line. This will mean a distant cousin has rights similar to a son. Sacrifices will be made and inconvenience endured as long as a genealogical commonality can be demonstrated.

Regrettably, this loving care seldom crosses over to those outside the family.

Overall, Bengalis are a law-abiding and non-violent people. Security was almost non-existent in our dwellings. We only experienced one break-in and never a physical assault. There was no real animosity directed against the missionary. In more recent years, two influences have begun to change this situation. During the civil war of 1971 the poetic temperament of the Bengali was replaced in many youths with a more aggressive, self-centered perspective on life. This has transferred to the political scene, where chaos often reigns. The other negative relates to the burgeoning Islamic Fundamentalism movement. Bengalis, in the past, have carried their Muslim allegiance rather lightly. Sufism (a mystical interpretation of Islam) traditionally has led Muslims into a more pluralistic, accepting attitude toward life. Sadly, this is beginning to change toward more rigidity and religious fanaticism.

Bengalis are a fun loving people. They enjoy laughing and seeing the lighter side of life. Their resilience is legendary. The Bengali Nobel Prize laureate Rabindranath Tagore wrote of the water lilies being subjected to the blowing wind and driving rain. Yes, the stems bend over with the onslaught of nature, sometimes even being covered with water. But, biding their time in a submissive posture, they await the passing of the storm. And then, with a fierce pride, they once again stand erect proclaiming to all their victory over adversity. This, says Tagore, is the Bengali. Cyclones, tornadoes, floods, famines, two presidential assassinations, and a devastating civil war have ravaged their land since independence in 1971. Bowed but not beaten. Giving assent to the doctrine of Allah's sovereignty and possessing an overwhelming instinct to survive, they fall and rise. Such, they say, is their *kopal*, which literally means forehead, but refers to fate.

Lyndi

Being a compulsively organized person, it will not come as a surprise that our one and only child came into our lives as per exact schedule, i.e., in the cool season just after our language exams were completed. We were grateful that a 40 mile road with only two river crossings by ferry had been constructed, connecting Manikganj to Dhaka. This cut our travel time by bus to around three hours.

Julie went to the Catholic Holy Family Hospital in Dhaka two weeks prior to the projected birth date. This was our first serious separation, and I found it rather excruciating. Our Southern Baptist missionary friends, Pat and Betty Johnson, who lived in the capital city, were of major assistance to us.

The day before the due date, February 6, 1965, I could no longer restrain myself. Making my way from Manikganj to the hospital, I was stricken with the usual first-father anxiety syndrome. With great delight, I learned that Julie had just commenced labor. Between painful contractions, we had tender moments of expressed love and commitment. The tape recorder quietly playing in the background added sanctity and assurance to the scene as it played "God Will Take Care of You." In prayer we claimed the Lord's protection over Julie and our soon-to-be-born child.

When the time came for Julie to be moved to the labor and delivery room, my request to accompany here there was denied. I have always regretted missing that, for me, once in a lifetime experience. After an uncomfortable night, Julie produced a healthy, beautiful baby girl whom we name Linda Sue (Lyndi, for short). A certain amount of instantaneous maturity takes place as you first gaze upon a human being which you had a part in bringing into this world. My personal frame of reference had completed a trinity of focus. First self; then husband; and now father. Wow! Awesome. Never would life be the same. Never!

Seven days after her birth, we took Lyndi back to Manikganj where a tumultuous welcome awaited her—another first for this placid village. A white-skinned infant! We never lacked for a baby-sitter.

India

In August of 1965, Julie and I with six-month-old Lyndi and the Fosters, who had sailed to Pakistan with us, set off on the four day train trek to the cool mountains of South India. It was standard procedure to take a vacation away from the intense heat of East

Pakistan for six weeks a year. There was no suitable place for such a break within the country.

Our journey took us through the compacted masses of the hopeless in the most depressing city on the face of the earth, Calcutta. Everywhere—emaciated beggars; everywhere—eight-foot-square hovels set up on the sidewalks for families of eight; everywhere—car horns producing a cacophony which jars the innermost soul; everywhere—nauseating smells of urine and defecation; everywhere—the assaults of germ-laden flies and mosquitoes. And worst of all, there is no escape from everywhere. It surrounds, it infiltrates, it strangles. Everywhere is everywhere. "O Calcutta, there is no escape from your pervasive grip, except the escape of *Kali*, the goddess of death for whom your city is named. Escape into nowhere. Final escape from everywhere."

Three nights on an Indian train, traveling third-class in a three-tier-bunk sleeper car, is a series of horrors. Hard slats battered every vulnerable bone. While traveling, the cooling breezes were mixed with coal soot which constantly bombarded the eyes and stuck to sweaty skin. When stopped, the train became a giant oven, slowly baking hundreds of perspiring victims. The not so gentle swaying of the moving train transformed teetotalers into apparent drunkards as they sought to navigate the crowded aisles. And then there were the "bathrooms." Often without water and always smelly, they were simply holes that emptied out onto the tracks.

But the end of the journey made it all worthwhile. The Nilgiri Hills are near Mysore. Chugging slowly up into the majestic Nilgiri range in an open train car was pure joy. Sweaters were brought out. Memories of recent purgatory-like experiences were quickly blotted out by breathing the fresh, clean air, seeing the stately trees, smelling the blooming flowers pregnant with heavenly fragrance, and hearing the symphonic strains of the choirs of wild birds. The senses came alive. A foretaste of paradise.

The missionary guest homes were wonderfully relaxing and rejuvenating. Three ample meals a day, plus two tea breaks produced the effect of an all day feast. We were even served breakfast in our room by tall, turbaned Indian "bearers." The quiet walks through mountain lanes always produced awe-inspiring vistas.

But storm clouds were on the horizon. India and Pakistan (East and West) hovered on the very precipice of war. Each side damned the other with inflammatory rhetoric. Within days the forces of destruction were unleashed. It became quickly evident that India would be the victor. Most of the fighting took place on West Pakistan soil. Reports, however, indicated the situation was extremely tense in the East. We learned that John and Joan Laurence, who were overseeing the Bible Correspondence School in our absence, had packed our goods in drums and then permanently evacuated to London. That left no one of our mission in the eastern province of the country. Foreign embassies were strongly advising the withdrawal of all "non-essential personnel" in East Pakistan. In light of this upheaval, and other personal issues, the Fosters decided to resign from the mission and return to the States. This left Julie and me as the only ones of our group actively assigned to East Pakistan. Mary Macdonald had been transferred to South India.

Our leaders offered us the option of going to West Pakistan as missionaries because the work was more established and stable there. This had no appeal to us whatsoever. Alternatively we could work with Gospel Recordings in Bangalore (near the CIGM headquarters) for some weeks until the situation clarified. So, with a distinct lack of enthusiasm, I became a "packer" in the Gospel Recordings warehouse. We lived on their compound with the bachelor director. Our tiny room with a bunk bed did not add any luster to life.

The one highlight of this frustrating period was the opportunity to be the guest speaker at an Inter-varsity sponsored youth retreat in Mysore City, South India. While speaking at the final session, I was totally frozen with nervous tension. There seemed to be absolutely no way to continue speaking. Just as I was ready to accept the embarrassment of failure and sit down, the Lord gave an infusion of grace and help. I pressed on and was able to give an invitation. At the end, six young people gave their lives to Christ. One of those students went on to become a full-time Christian worker in South India. Over thirty years later he continues on in the ministry. How grateful I am that God's mercy was proved adequate in the crucible of emotional weakness.

Return Home

The security situation in East Pakistan remained unstable. Lyndi was just nine months old, but we pushed the mission for permission to return. With more than a bit of hesitation they acquiesced, with the proviso that we give a written statement absolving them of all responsibility for our safety. This we were glad to do. Because the India/Pakistan border was still closed, we undertook the return journey through Sri Lanka, where we were forced to spend a week in Colombo because of a delayed flight and a missed ongoing connection.

On December 24, 1965, we three wayfaring pilgrims arrived back in Manikganj. There was absolutely no outward celebration for Lyndi's first Christmas. We spent the day cleaning our house and unpacking drums. Though the political crisis remained, we were delighted to be "home" and freed up to engage in what we strongly felt was God's will for us.

Our most traumatic "moment" in East Pakistan involved Lyndi and our kerosene fan. One evening, before retiring for the night, I went into Lyndi's small room and filled the burner with kerosene. She was sleeping in her crib just two feet away from the fan. After I finished, I stood up and my *lungi* (a skirt-like cloth Bengali men wear in their homes) caught on the fan and tipped it over. Immediately fiery kerosene spread over the floor inches away from Lyndi's bed. I began yelling "FIRE" at the top of my voice, grabbed 18 month-old Lyndi, and thrust her into Julie's arms. Telling them to get out, I ran to the bathroom and tried to lift the huge clay water container. It broke apart in my hands, spilling gallons of precious water down the drain.

The flames were now engulfing the room. I yanked a curtain off of a door and tried to beat the fire out but this cloth soon flared up and came perilously close to setting my *lungi* alight. Neighbors were all screaming out to know if Lyndi was safe.

Knowing time was definitely not on my side, I tried to mentally evaluate the relative value of seeking to put out the fire or just getting important items out of the house before it went up in flames. Suddenly I remembered a large container of boiled drinking water in the kitchen. Fortunately it was full. I grabbed it and threw it into Lyndi's room, Amazingly, it subdued the major part of the fire. Scores of Bengalis appeared with buckets of water and quickly the once all-consuming flames were totally extinguished. Our village fire truck appeared about ten minutes later.

Lyndi's room was smoke-filled and wooden items were charred. The three of us, much later, lay together on our bed and profusely thanked the Lord for His grace and protection. The next morning we took inventory and found that not one item had been stolen by the 75 or so Muslim and Hindu Bengali neighbors that had swarmed through our darkened home the night before.

Another crisis of the first term related to Sheila Archer, middle-aged, single missionary, who had been assigned to Manikganj. Sheila was a veteran servant of the Lord, having spent several terms with our mission in South India.

One day, during the searing heat of April, Sheila sent word to us that we should go to her house, because she was beginning to experience paralysis in her left leg. Upon seeing her, Julie suggested the possibility of polio, for which Sheila had never been vaccinated. Sheila discarded the idea because she didn't think she could get it at her age.

Over the next few days the paralysis continued to intensify and spread to her other leg. Evacuation to Dhaka seemed to be advised. That was to be no easy task, as Sheila could no longer walk. She was able to sit up in the bus, but at the two ferries we used a folding camp cot and coolies to transport her the necessary distances that we would normally walk. After many hassles of changing from ferry to bus to three-wheeled "baby taxi," we were able to get her installed in a room at the Catholic hospital. The doctors gravely told us it was polio and that the virus would just have to run its course. They did have an iron lung available if the polio began to affect Sheila's lungs.

Much prayer was made over the next few days that God would touch and heal. Amazingly the virus was confined to her legs. But we had to arrange a medical evacuation by plane (with stretcher space) to London. After many months of therapy, Sheila was able to return to Manikganj to resume ministry for another term.

Spirituality

Those Manikganj "lost" years, when we had not one convert or even a serious inquirer, were absolutely essential in the process of building a solid foundation for our marriage, family, and ministry. Particularly meaningful were the following arenas in which personal development took place:

Spirituality was being formed within the matrix of failure. I was being weaned away from self-sufficiency and reliance on natural gifts. My periods of moodiness were particularly difficult for Julie. When upset, for whatever insignificant reason, my response would be to simply cut off communication. Actually this reaction to irritation seemed to be beyond my control. It would last from a few hours up to an overnight. Misery would engulf me as, in bed, I would turn my back to Julie and seek to find release through sleep. My temperamental bent toward melancholy is certainly a key factor in this recurring tendency toward depression. Unfortunately, I have not found total release, but by God's grace it has greatly lessened. My regret is for the unintended hurt it brought to Julie, and to a lesser extent, to Lyndi.

Perhaps my pride was somewhat moderated by my excursion into obscurity. But, actually I kind of doubt it. Building up the Bible Correspondence School into a recognized cooperative force for evangelism throughout the country fed my ego and fueled my secret thoughts of personal grandeur. Amazing how self and service can get so intertwined.

Another area of highlighted failure during those years was my impatience. Having always been a fast eater, I developed an aversion to sitting at the dining table for longer than five to seven minutes. When my meal was consumed, I would leave and go engage in a more productive activity, like a siesta, if it was midday. Amazing patience was displayed by Julie, as she never nagged me. She just waited out the years until I would become convicted of such insensitive behavior. Many other illustrations of this temperamental inadequacy could be cited, but I don't have the patience to engage in the necessary exercise of recall!

When one wholeheartedly desires to follow the path of purity, why does the Romans 7 conflict of flesh and spirit often dominate? By God's grace I have never touched another woman in lust since my marriage to Julie. Likewise, I have never made an emotional advance toward any other woman for my personal gratification. Yet, the struggle for mental purity has never ceased. At times like a tiger roaring for ascendancy and total dominance; at other times just lurking quietly in the shadows, waiting for an opportunity to pounce; yet seemingly always there, always there. Unrelenting. For the record, let it be stated, I have every intention to stay engaged in the battle, and by the Lord's powerful enabling, to make it to the end having been a faithful husband and father and Christian.

Lest I be overly introspective on the down side, let me brighten the picture by declaring the joys of having an immersion experience into the one flesh reality expounded by Scripture. Manikganj afforded Julie and me ample time to develop together into what I would call a passionate relationship. To be accurate, I would have to say there were some months in the mid-70's when my emotions cooled down. But my will was unshakable. Without informing anyone of my perplexity, I just waited for my emotions to come into sync with my will. They did.

On the human level, Julie has consistently been my emotional ballast. She has encountered each trial with an amazing equilibrium. As a wife, mother, secretary, gourmet cook, and hospitality expert, Julie has never faltered in excellence. In fact, it is almost impossible to define a sin of commission in her life. Such has been the Lord's special gift to me.

Likewise, our joy was deepened with the coming of Lyndi into our home. Though she was an easy child to raise, still my selfishness was challenged many times and in many ways over the years. We (with the emphasis on me) made a considered decision to limit our family to one child in light of the difficult ministry to which we felt called. There were times when Lyndi would gently complain, but then quickly acquiesce when we reminded her of the "extras" she received in life by being a special focus within a small nuclear family—like tagging along with us to visit and/or minister in 35 countries.

Growing up in a home of quasi-poverty set the initial stage for my view on lifestyle issues. This was reinforced by OM and our first term of voluntary identification with the poor and deprived. Somehow we have always had more money than we have needed for personal expenses. This has allowed us to share ample sums of money over the years with the needy.

We have never owned property and do not plan to, at least in this life. Not sure if we will have a title to our reserved "mansion" in Heaven or not. No chance of inheritance. Our two sets of parents died without having enough to write a will for. In fact, we helped pay burial expenses for the last one on each side of the family.

Until the age of 54, I had been committed to a "no savings" policy. But then a close friend gently admonished me in light of what Julie would have to survive on if I died first, which is basically the Social Security allowance plus a small amount for rent. So, I now struggle a bit with guilt as each month an amount is set aside as savings.

By no stretch of the imagination are we deprived. A "simple lifestyle" is so relative. With whom are we being compared? What really is a biblical standard on the subject? The answers vary tremendously. In the end, each believer will have to work through this difficult subject in light of so many variables. But I do wish the affluent could spend considerable time with the "poorest of the poor" and then, in prayer, struggle with the issue of setting a personal standard of lifestyle.

Our first term definitely broadened me as far as accepting the wider perimeters of the body of Christ. Over the years it has been a wonderful privilege to fellowship intimately with evangelicals within all kinds of denominations. Such a rich diversity!

Ingrained in my mind is a confrontation I had with a senior missionary of great repute in Bangladesh. Without doubt he was a sincere, devout, and true Christian. One problem. He did not articulate his belief in the inerrancy of Scripture quite like Tennessee Temple College did. He was from the United Kingdom, and I have found that overall, the British could care less about formulating tight, dogmatic creedal statements.

But, inerrancy! That was the all-essential issue upon which Christianity stands or crumbles. After all, the domino theory of one fall and the rest will inevitably collapse, must surely apply to the king of the dominos, i.e., inerrancy. So, appropriately, I felt, I launched a "jihad" against my Christian brother. Missionaries and national leaders were warned of heresy in the camp. Excommunication, or at least exclusion, was my well-publicized stand. After all, it is important to stand. Right?

Well, yes and no. I still today concur with inerrancy but, no, I no longer launch "jihads" against those who may frame their devout beliefs a bit differently from me. After dropping my verbal bombs of destruction on the British missionary, I became deeply convicted of my lack of love and sensitivity. On an unforgettable morning, I profusely apologized to a gracious and forgiving Christian brother. How clean I felt after that meeting.

And finally, my first term gave me ample opportunity to frame and work out my personal doctrine of perseverance in adversity. How easy to cut and run when expectations are not met. How reassuring to always maintain an escape route. No burned bridges. Options always open. But, the problem is, that is not the model we find in the walk of Jesus toward the Cross. Or, more on a totally human level, Paul consistently gave us an example of forward movement regardless of the cost.

I used to meditate frequently on the words of the chorus, "I have decided to follow Jesus… The Cross before me, the world behind me. No turning back. No turning back." I had considered the cost, I had put my hand to the plow. Now, onward and forward. Nothing less would be worthy of my high calling in Christ Jesus.

And such was our first term.

Chapter 6

Darkening Clouds

How do I feel about furloughs and deputation? Guess you could say it is a love-hate relationship. The love part focuses on being with warm, gracious, loving supporters who have had an indispensable part in our ministry through prayer and gifts. During visits it is a joy to seek to enter into their lives and become more cognizant of their concerns. Most of our churches and individual supporters have remained with us throughout our time in Asia.

We had a small part in ministry to a Swiss couple with an NGO (Non-Government Organization) who had been assigned to Bangladesh. Upon return to Switzerland, they commenced giving over $300 a month for our support. What an encouragement it was for us to be in their lovely home and to tour a portion of the Swiss Alps with them in 1989. Another couple of moderate means are in their 80's. The wife is on the down side of Alzheimer's. Yet, their $50 continues to come in as it has for the past 30 years. Humbling indeed.

I would be remiss if I did not enunciate a few of the many things our home church, Highland Park Baptist of Southfield, Michigan, has done for us. From 1962, they have met one third of our annual financial requirements. Four lovely apartments on the church grounds are maintained for furloughing missionaries. Even linens and kitchen utensils are provided. The only charge is for long distance phone calls. For many years they provided cars for use on furlough. Presently, folk in the church often lend a car to those on short visits. Schooling for the missionary kids is available at subsidized rates in the church's Southfield Christian School. Parcels or substantial monetary gifts are sent to the one hundred adults (along with their children) on the missionary roster each year. Other needs are met from the annual missionary conference special offering. Most of all, one experiences a warmth and acceptance from the parishioners, even though Highland Park is a large church (2,000 members) filled with above average income parishioners. The Sunday morning services are rapturous, with worshipful anthems and solid biblical teaching. Julie and I are intensely grateful for the privilege of being part of such a great body of believers.

The "hate" portion of the home assignment equation relates to the hassles of extensive travel and frequent sermonizing. It is all too much compressed into too short a time. Teaching is more of a challenge and joy to me than repetitively preaching a missions sermon. Probably the reason relates to the stimulating interaction I experience with sharp seminary students. There is always a freshness in dialogue even though I have taught the same basic credit course on Muslim Evangelism at least twenty times.

People. My profession is all about people. In all shapes, sizes, and commitments. Some I enjoy, some I endure. Without a doubt, I engender the same reaction from those who first encounter me. There is within me a propensity toward shyness and a desire for quietness. Meeting a lot of unknown folk is extremely difficult. My rejuvenation in life comes from lying on the bed and thinking, away from the crowds.

I can be aggressive, stubborn, and dominant in dealing with people. These fruits of the flesh within my personality militate against the deeper spiritual experience for which I long. Many are the apologies I have made over the years for my insensitivities toward sensitive people. My goal is to overwhelm the flesh with the spirit. 1 Corinthians 13 is the Bible's most convicting passage for me personally. But I am afraid love is all too often neutralized through my drive and impatience.

Home Assignment

During our first home assignment in 1967-68, we traveled over 30,000 miles and I spoke in 200 meetings. That was the first and last time I subjected myself to such an overload of people and speaking engagements. From then on I studied on furloughs or have just taken three month tours to our supporting churches on four year cycles.

The highlight of our initial furlough was the recruitment of Ed and Irene Welch. This special couple labored in Bangladesh under adverse conditions for twelve years. Ed is presently serving in the personnel department of SIM USA. Everyone needs friends who have unreserved commitment on a reciprocal basis, friendship that not only supports but also rebukes when necessary. The Lord has given us this kind of support system with the Welches.

Family relationships on the Miami side continued to be strained. My brother Jimmy was doing well in his ornamental iron business. He, however, basically ignored his "fanatical" brother. Dad, ever the dreamer, was busy inventing a welding holder with a switch, an innovation which he was confident would bring him fame and riches. Mom was the exception with her warmth and graciousness. She thoroughly enjoyed her three-year-old granddaughter even though she was frustrated by the fact that Lyndi spoke more Bengali than English. There was, within my family, always a realization that I could not be too far off the wall if I could convince such a beautiful person as Julie to marry me. They so appreciated her quiet, gentle, and sweet spirit.

A tapestry will be a beautiful work of art as long as the appropriate gifted artist is at work. But the potential of an outside force of destruction is an ever present reality. Someone can possibly intervene and cause the design to be inhibited or wander off in unorthodox directions. Thus the symmetry is ruined. Such also can be the fate of the human tapestry.

And this is how it could have happened. Our small International Christian Fellowship (ICF, as the name had been changed by now) office in Wheaton, Illinois, was overseen by our home director and one secretary. I remember being impressed by the director's tastefully decorated office. His huge well-cushioned, black, executive chair gave forth an air of imperial grandeur.

Then, one day, this thirty-year-old budding missionary was propositioned: Would I become the ICF associate director, with the understanding that the big chair would be mine within a year or two when the present sixty-five-year-old "in charge" would be retiring?

Very quickly I was fantasizing that those tough days of East Pakistan were all behind me. Soon I would be walking the corridors of power with other Interdenominational Foreign Missions Association heavies. My precious wife and daughter would be rescued from the frustrations of one of the poorest countries in the world and brought to live in a comfortable suburban home in the evangelical *Mecca* of America. There would be exciting scope for my gifts, great potential for fruitfulness in ministry, not to mention (at least openly) the probable recognition I would receive.

All I needed was to declare the Lord's imprimatur on my fantasies and I was home free! After all, was not such an offer by my superiors in the faith a confirmation that I should submit and accept? Certainly this is a pattern I have noted among believers. Mobility (defined as the "Lord's will") is almost always upward. Really an interesting phenomenon, is it not, how God almost never "leads" downward? Yet He modeled such a "descent" in Christ (Phil. 2). Have we somehow gotten our heavenly signals crossed and ended up moving in the wrong direction? Worth pondering, I think.

And so it was, at an immature age, I was faced with a struggle between the flesh and the spirit. Advice from the American saints came down strongly on the side of "multiplying" myself through recruitment efforts as U.S. Director. Family on the home side was delighted at the thought of our daughter growing up in a culturally appropriate environment. Then there was (and is) my natural bent to enjoy ease and shun deprivation. Since I am a Westerner, I would have to be a masochist to be excited about the lifestyle available in a place like East Pakistan. And such a person I am not.

There was only one problem. God's calling to Muslim evangelism still burned deeply in my soul. In reality, I had hardly begun the battle. How could I just walk away from what I so intensely felt was God's will?

Settled! We would go back to East Pakistan.

The above meditation does not make me any kind of spiritual hero. It is just that I have a compelling desire to stay engaged in front line warfare for the Lord as long as possible. To the best of my ability in discerning God's will, this appears to be His direction. Julie and Lyndi have been completely supportive of me in this pilgrimage.

Initial temptations are always the most difficult to deal with. Once a Goliath is faced down, other enemies are as grasshoppers. A number of potentially enticing offers have come and gone—director of a well-known mission; dean of a university's program of intercultural studies; head of a Muslim think tank; etc. By God's grace the battle was won in 1968. No longer does the siren call to "success" create dissonance in my soul. In fact, I no longer even pray over such offers.

Now does that mean the drive for personal recognition has been totally subdued? No way. I still find fulfillment and joy in any acknowledgment, written or oral, that comes my way. But the temptation to leave Asia for higher profile or more lucrative positions was dealt with at that watershed moment on our first furlough.

Dhaka

In consultation with the mission, it had been decided we would move to Dhaka, the capital city, for our second term. The correspondence school had outgrown the village of Manikganj. A large house was rented which served as the school's office (in the living-dining room area), mission guest house, and our personal home. It was a place where happy memories were made as Lyndi spent five of her impressionable growing-up years there.

The correspondence school soon became a thriving outreach. We had a number of Bengali employees. Branch schools were commenced with cooperating missions. Follow-up rallies for advanced students were held throughout the country. Muslims were being presented with the Word of God as never before.

Simultaneously, I was involved with a number of other ministries. A group of us started an annual spiritual life conference for all missionaries and nationals who understood English. Speakers like Alan Redpath, John Stott, and Anglican Archbishop Marcus Loane shared insights with the spiritually hungry. Books from the West were made available by the Association of Baptist for World Evangelism book shop. Those days were the highlight of each year.

Operation Mobilization (OM) was sponsored into the country by our team. Their ship Logos made two ministry tours to Bangladesh. Over the ensuing years this group of Christian revolutionaries made an overwhelmingly positive contribution in Bangladesh. It was always a privilege for us to share our home with George Verwer during his frequent visits.

For an extended period I edited a monthly bulletin which was a vehicle for sharing news and prayer requests among the missionary community. Hospitality was an important part of Julie's life. Christian workers from around the country would come to Dhaka and stay with us while they did necessary work in the capital. Counseling missionaries and nationals was a fulfilling ministry for me.

During this second term I was asked to travel to rural churches and speak on revival and evangelism. This was part of a cooperative effort by most of the country's church and mission organizations. It was a joy to be immersed into the language and culture of the Christian community. Many nights we slept on mud church floors in remote villages.

My feelings about traditional Bangladesh Christians are a bit ambivalent. Many are descendants of converts from William Carey's time, mostly from Hindu background. Power plays within the various denominations are common. Intelligent Christians scramble towards the top with little focus on the teaching of Christ concerning servant leadership. Ego seems to be the dominant driving force in the upward spin toward recognition. Regrettably, lay-believers are, at times, prone to be less than discerning when it comes to making a distinction between natural and spiritual gifts as they choose their leaders. The power person with charisma ends up with great authority and influence over many churches and pastors. But, sadly, he may have little or no spiritual qualifications for the task.

Fortunately, that is not the whole picture. Thousands of average Bengali Christians live their lives and bear the Name with more than average grace, considering their poverty and their hostile, Islamic surroundings. And some leaders excel. Simon Sircar was my Bangladesh Christian mentor. At that time he was pastor of one of the most influential churches in the country. At present he is the principal of a large cooperative theological college. Simon is a powerful, articulate, preacher of God's Word. His theological insights have been sharpened by taking graduate degrees in the Philippines and the States. But what strikes one most about Simon is his unpretentious manner. He is totally unaffected by popularity, acclaim, and an earned doctorate. His life serves as an ongoing gentle rebuke to my pride.

Unfortunately, many of the problems of the church's dependency on foreign funds can be laid at the feet of missionaries. From the time of William Carey, who came from England in 1792 to commence work among the Bengalis, there has been a major flow of financial assistance to the believers. How sad that the Christians have not been able, over the generations, to escape the devastating cycle of ongoing poverty.

Recurrent Tragedies

Yes, Bengalis seem forever caught in a *karma* of tragedy. Yes, both on a national and an individual level, these people have developed a dependency complex that undermines personal initiative. Yes, many feel the affluent West is obligated to share their wealth with them.

Now, where is the way out? Back up. The prior question has to be, "Is there a way out?" After living in Bangladesh for twenty years, I just really do not know. It is true there is a resilience among these people of sorrow. But it is at bare survival level. And it is accomplished with massive external Western government and non-government aid. The millions of dollars never solve the problem, rather, they just prolong existence within a milieu of deprivation.

Divine Threads Within A Human Tapestry

Western Christians know they are commanded to be caring. A real believer cannot pass by those who are suffering without stopping to bandage their wounds. The cry of the hungry and thirsty must not go unheeded. Christ exhorts all to be their brother's keeper.

It is difficult, however, to incarnate such lofty words. One terribly stormy afternoon in Dhaka as I drove along the suburban streets I could hardly see twenty feet ahead of me in the pelting rainstorm. My "lofty" mission had been to procure some last-minute needed items for our missionary fellowship meal that would take place in a few hours. I was in a hurry, as usual. One of my greater sanctification struggles focuses on a car's accelerator. The slippery road was in an adversarial relationship with my goal of swift accomplishment of the task I was engaged in.

In a fleeting moment, I saw a form with crumpled clothes in a fetal position laid out by the side of the road. Bangladesh was, at that time, in the grip of a Book of Lamentations-type famine. Villagers had come by the tens of thousands to Dhaka to either find employment or beg. Literally scores swooned in the streets from malnutrition.

In the next few seconds as I sped by, many contradictory thoughts bombarded my mind. "Yes, I am in a hurry; no, not in that big of a hurry. He is but one of hundreds; he is important to God. I am a 'priest;' I am about to pass by on the other side. My wife is going to make a feast tonight; this guy is starving. I have nice clothes; he has rags. I am warm and dry; he is soaked to the skin and cold. I have hope; he has no hope."

Brakes applied. Sliding to a stop, I reversed, got out in the rain and helped an amazed creation of God get into the car. At our home he was fed, clothed and put to bed. The next morning we gave him money and urged him to return to his loved ones in his village.

But how many others are "passed by"? Impossible, utterly impossible to meet every need in Bangladesh, much less throughout a world filled with the destitute and forsaken. And so, there is a hole dug deep into my soul, a hole of darkness that is so intense that the absence of light is, at times, feelable, painfully feelable.

One might ask when did this heightened sensitivity to suffering take place? As usual in my life, I can pinpoint crisis moments with some degree of accuracy.

Friday the 13th of November, 1970.

The Bay of Bengal is a natural conduit for hurricanes to traverse before slamming into the southern coast of Bangladesh. During a cool Thursday evening we heard radio reports of a huge hurricane starting to pummel the coastal region. We were not overly concerned as we had a solid house and Dhaka is a few hundred miles inland. For us it was a moderately stormy night.

Fast-forward ten days. I am standing on a dirt embankment looking out over the tranquil Bay of Bengal. Behind me is a desolate plain, raped of crops, trees, bamboo huts, and most sadly, of men, women, and children. The few survivors told me the story of a night of savage plunder.

There was no real warning system in place. A few people had transistor radios (no electricity) and heard of the oncoming hurricane. But there was no place to flee. They hunkered down and waited. Thousands of day laborers had come into the area from further inland. It was harvest time, and they could earn much needed rupees by cutting rice stalks in the daytime and sleeping in a lean-to at night. They were totally vulnerable.

Billowing black clouds rolled in. Rain and wind, first as delicate and welcome as a visit from a close friend, slowly changed into a fearsome, roaring, all-consuming Bengal tiger. Thunder clamored in antiphonal rhythm across the plain. Lightening streaked the sky, looking awesomely like the finger of God directing a great and terrible symphony of tragedy.

For eight hours, chaos reigned. A wall of sea water had churned up into a twenty-foot-high tower of annihilation that pushed miles inland, obliterating all that stood in its path. Shanties collapsed. Mothers held on tightly to their babies and sought to grab the tops of trees as they fought to stay above the swirling water. Cries to Allah of despair and panic vied for supremacy over the howling forces of nature gone berserk.

Towards dawn the surging sea returned homeward. Left in its wake were dazed survivors as well as bloated bodies of men, women, children, and animals. Eternity had come calling on Black Friday the thirteenth. Its quota of 500,000 for East Pakistan had gruesomely been filled.

As I stood on the embankment, I noticed scores of banana stalks had been recently planted into the top and sides of the raised soil. An elderly, bearded Muslim unlocked the mystery. With downcast eyes he soberly recalled that terrifying next morning when the bereaved sought out the bodies of their loved ones. Without ceremony, pits were dug into the embankment and bodies were committed to their creator. Banana trees served for markers as well as mute reminders that life struggles to prevail over death.

The highest percentage of the dead were women, children, and the aged. They were the ones unable to defy the storm's overpowering strength by holding onto treetops for hours. As far as we were able to ascertain, all of the dead were Muslims or Hindus. Not one Christian among them.

An awesome configuration of events took place that mid-November. It was full moon, high tide, and the storm came in at night. Then there were the thousands of other workers who had come into the coastal region for harvest time. All of these were negative factors that dramatically caused the death toll to soar. The gurus of statistics have declared this 1970 hurricane as having killed more people than any other natural catastrophe in the twentieth century.

An onlooking world gasped in horror. Within days relief supplies began pouring into East Pakistan. Christian agencies, most of them reputable (though not all), took up headquarters in Dhaka. I guess my biggest struggle with this "invasion" was the high profile of some of the Christian workers. For a few, their choice of residence was the lone five-star hotel in Dhaka. After the ensuing civil war, one group brought in a movie star to assist in their fund raising efforts. I began to wonder if human tragedy was being turned into a product which would "sell" well in the West and thus assure an agency's financial well being.

One of the most dedicated and zealous of all missionaries I have ever been privileged to meet is Southern Baptist Jim McKinley. Within days, Jim had organized a much needed operation of sinking tube wells in the disaster area. I was graciously allowed by Jim to assist for a few days. Getting up at 4:30 AM, we left his base in Feni and traveled south for two hours (65 miles) in Jim's Landrover. It was in this context that I found myself standing on the embankment, pondering, reflecting, hurting.

"God, you are the Omnipotent One. You alone control the rotation of the moon, the boundaries of the tides, the wind, and the rain. Are not hurricanes within the purview of your sovereignty and authority? Who, but You, is responsible for what I see? God, are You hurting as I am? Are You listening to the wails of those who lost their father... wife... beloved child? Can You see these banana stalks... and the ten-day-old decaying corpses beneath them? Is it possible for You to remember that these very bones eleven days ago were infants at a mother's breast, children dancing in abandoned gaiety, and elders pondering the meaning of the universe? Lord, give me a word of insight, of assurance, of grace. Please."

The moment was sacred. A gorgeous sunset was taking place before my eyes. As the sun dipped further into the western sky, great rays of light played hide and seek in and out of the silver-lined clouds. Slowly they diminished in intensity as they made their way back to source and were then totally absorbed into the setting sun.

And darkness covered the face of East Pakistan.

In like manner, humans made from dust must return to dust. The cycle of new life and inevitable death moves relentlessly on throughout the millennia. Life is ever so fragile, only ever a split second away from cessation.

And it seemed the Lord said to me, "My son, this is the rhythm of the universe. Move on in faith and fidelity to My Word. Keep pressing on with tenacity. One blessed future day, your innumerable questions will be dealt with. Until then, press on."

But, the "black hole in my soul" still bothers me, reinforced ever so frequently by further incidents of suffering and pain. Sorry, but the glib panaceas so often coldly articulated from Western pulpits leave me barren. These pontifications seem to lack a sensitivity to the hunger pains and the emotional distresses of my people. So, for over a quarter of a century, I have "pressed on in faith" since that memorable occasion in East Pakistan. But never far from my cognitive processes and emotional responses is an ongoing theological and pragmatic battle between query and faith.

And that brings us to the next great tragedy of Bangladesh.

Chapter 7

Civil War: The Beginning

The launch sliced its way through the calm waters of one of the many wide rivers in inland East Pakistan. A full moon created reflections of stately coconut trees projecting out from the river bank onto the shimmering water. A radio provided a touch of romance to the scene as it played folk songs depicting the life of fishermen toiling on the rivers.

Into this scene of tranquility insert two launch passengers, myself and a young Bengali university student. It was early in my missionary career and I was keen to learn as much about my newly adopted country as I could. My animated informant told me a story of colonialistic oppression and deprivation.

India, including what later became East and West Pakistan, had been ruled by the British for over two centuries. Finally, more out of exhaustion than conviction, the British capitulated in 1947 and allowed the nations of India and Pakistan (East and West) to come into existence. With this "Partition," India would be a secular state while Pakistan, with an overwhelming Muslim majority, would have an Islamic governmental bias. The two wings of the one country of Pakistan were located on the far eastern and far western sides of India, separated from each other by a distance of 1,200 miles.

Soon after independence, the fragile ideological-cum-religious bonds that held the two wings of Pakistan together began to unravel. The Bengalis of the East, small in stature, were poets, musicians, and more Sufi in their mystical-oriented devotion to Allah. Across the

Indian sub-continent the Punjabis, Sindhis, Pathans, and other ethnic West Pakistanis were tall, aggressive people with a dogmatic belief in the tenants of Islam.

By several million, the majority population resided in the East. However, the central government control of the whole nation was totally in the West. Thus, the Bengalis felt that, after finally overthrowing a white colonial power, they had once again been subjugated, this time by a domineering, brown skinned, alien Muslim force. And they were not happy.

After my intellectual student acquaintance related the above, he paused and, with great strength of conviction, said, "No, no, it shall not continue. We will overthrow these neo-colonialists. Our nation will one day be free. We are destined to breathe the fresh air of freedom. Bangladesh (Country of the Bengalis) will soon be a reality. You just wait and see. Mark my words."

And so I waited and I saw. From our earliest days there, we observed anti-government protests. The favorite *modus operandi* was to call a *hartal* which basically was an enforced strike shutting down the city or, in some instances, the whole country. All shops and offices were to be kept shut, either through choice or strong intimidation. No transport was allowed on the road. These strikes, which occurred frequently, were for a duration of between six hours and two days. They were a major inconvenience to the general populace and an acute embarrassment to the government. Violence often accompanied the *hartals*. Secularized students were usually in the forefront of the organized opposition. Even though the Bengalis strongly desired independence, their aspirations were held in check by a well fortified army which was led by competent West Pakistani officers.

All that was lacking was a man of the soil with colossal charisma and mobilizing ability. In the late 60's this man walked onto the stage of history. Sheikh Mujibur Rahman was born to farmer parents in a most remote area of the interior of East Pakistan. What he lacked in education he made up in his powerful persona. His emotional speeches mesmerized the masses. He was only nominal in his devotion to Islam. Politically he was a pragmatist with leftist leanings. Oh, how the people loved him. His commands were obligations to be followed by the millions. A free and just election in February 1971, was clearly won by the Sheikh. The West Pakistani politicians were stunned. They thought they were in control of the voting process. Even though the population of the West was a minority, these politicians gave absolutely no thought to capitulating to that "rabble rouser Sheikh in the East."

Thus, a "historical moment" dawned for the Bengali masses. Their demand was simple. The Sheikh must rule a unified East and West Pakistan or the East would secede and go it alone. The answer from the West was a resounding, "No way!"

The Sheikh toured the Bengali countryside bringing out crowds of hundreds of thousands. In March, 1971, he made a startling announcement. Bengalis were told to no longer pay taxes to the central government. This was the last straw for the power men of the West. A massive weapons and personnel build-up had been going on for months. The army was poised, ready to put down the insurrection. Bengalis were prepared to fight back, but they had only full-throated slogans and bamboo sticks. No contest, not really. A bubble of fantasy was about to burst.

The Crackdown

The military made its dramatic move on the population of Dhaka on March 25, 1971. With lightening-like swiftness they arrested many of the leaders of the Awami League, the Sheikh's political party. A few were able to escape to India and set up a government-in-exile.

Amazingly, that night, I was able to tune into the military frequency on my small short-wave radio. How brazen the West Pakistanis were in that they chose to communicate in English over an open channel. Soon, I heard a gleeful officer excitedly announce, "We have the big bird in a cage." The Sheikh was taken in his home without resistance and flown immediately to West Pakistan where he sat out the next nine months of civil war in a prison cell. He had felt it would be cowardly to flee and take refuge in India. Such bravery almost cost him his life as most of the West Pakistani politicians wanted him tried and executed for treason. A few saner voices prevailed and the Sheikh continued on in solitary confinement.

Divine Threads Within A Human Tapestry

The 25th night was horrible: gun shots, artillery blasts, screams, and continuing radio reports by the army of new conquests and mass killings. I sat on the flat roof of our home emotionally distraught. Fires raged throughout the city. Our beloved people had gone to the precipice, and fallen over into perdition. Now, their political slogans had turned to cries of desperation for Allah to save them.

Radio and television stations were quickly commandeered. People were told to stay inside their homes and under no condition go out into the streets. I could hear simple barricades being put up by the students under cover of darkness. They did so at the risk of their lives.

Like everyone else, we had an Awami League mandated "Bangladesh flag" flying from our roof. Around 1 AM, I heard a platoon of soldiers coming down our road. As I peered over the railing of the roof, a soldier saw me and pointed his rifle at me. Miraculously, the Lord put it in his heart not to pull the trigger. I quickly retreated and took down the rebel flag. A close call!

After independence I went to the Bangladesh Television studio and was given a private showing of one of the tragic happenings of the night of March 25. Some brave person living in an apartment overlooking one of the University of Dhaka dorms filmed a mass killing. I could clearly see the military men gathering a large group of students together in an open courtyard. Some got on their knees with folded hands and begged the soldiers to spare their lives. Then the bullets began spraying into the chests and faces of these intellectual elite. One by one their bodies contorted as their souls took flight into eternity. Their only crime had been to love their country supremely. For that, they received an instant trial and execution.

Forty-eight hours after the carnage began, the people of Dhaka were allowed to go out to the markets for three hours only. Several of us missionaries, with camera in hand, commenced a tour of the city. Military trucks full of armed soldiers were patrolling many of the streets. We went straight to the University. There we met hysterical students who were anxious to guide us to the areas where atrocities had taken place. Most of the bodies had been buried or thrown into a nearby fast-flowing river. An exception was a huge heap of student corpses left behind a dorm, probably as an object lesson for any opposing remnant to ponder.

From the University we drove through the crowded old part of the city to the launch terminal. The Bengalis led us out to the large platform where the boats docked. On the 24th night scores of the homeless and beggars had taken shelter under the tin roof. Soldiers came, and in a senseless act of genocide, shot every man, woman, and child. Literally, the floor had been mopped with blood as the bodies were dragged to the edge of the platform and kicked into the river.

A few blocks down the road we came to a line of taxis. The drivers had been cowering on the floor of their cars when the military came and ordered them out. Bullets slammed into their bodies, transporting them into eternity. Muslims killed by fellow Muslims. Over and over the Bengali would express amazement and shock that a fellow believer in Allah could ever be guilty of such horrendous acts of violence.

Driving back toward our home, we saw a roadblock a few hundred yards ahead of us. I immediately turned off onto a side street and proceeded on a circuitous route that got us safely back to our home just before the reimposition of the curfew. We later heard that some foreigners had been out taking pictures as we had done. They were caught at a check point, taken to a military post, questioned with a great deal of vigor, and then ordered out of the country within 24 hours. We had barely missed such a fate.

Each day we were allowed to be outside our homes an hour or two longer. Within a week the curfew only applied to the hours of darkness. The city had been "secured." We kept hearing reports of the rural areas being totally controlled by the Bengalis. It was obvious, after a time of consolidation, the army would be moving out into the countryside. Stillness before the storm.

In early March (before the crackdown), I had sent in an extensive pro-Bengali article to the news section of Christianity Today. They published it in April with an update on the crackdown. If the Pakistani military had seen my biased report, I would either have been arrested or declared *persona-non-grata* and deported.

Fortunately for me, their readings did not extend to Christian periodicals. But I felt really good that the views of the oppressed had been presented to an influential, though limited, audience.

I desperately wanted to further share the details of the carnage even though there was a news blackout throughout the land. All foreign journalists had been expelled. One evening I made an audio tape of all that I had seen and heard. Very carefully, I wrapped it in plastic and concealed it under the soap in a shaving mug. Then I begged a development worker to take it with him when he left the country. He gave it serious consideration and eventually refused to take it as he felt it represented too great a personal risk.

Back to the exposed film. That definitely was a hot item. There was a strong possibility there would be door to door searches. We had hidden it behind a light switch on the wall. But even that could possibly be discovered. One of our team felt strongly the risk was too great to keep it. With great hesitation and no little sorrow, it was cut up and flushed down the toilet. No such search took place. Bad move.

Descent in Perdition

Evacuation time. Soon the word went out that all foreign embassies were strongly urging their people to leave for safe havens. Special planes came in to facilitate the withdrawal. It was a sad day when I visited the staging area and said farewell to perhaps ninety percent of all the missionaries who were resident in Dhaka. There was a deep level of hurt among many of the Christian nationals, who felt they were being deserted in their moment of crisis.

It was a tough call. We felt it best for our single lady, Dorothy McQuaker, to leave. A bit later, as conditions continued to deteriorate, it seemed wise to ask Bill and Anne Barnett, who had only been in the country a few months and didn't know Bengali, to fly over to West Pakistan to wait out the situation. This left Ed and Irene Welch along with Julie, our six-year-old Lyndi, and myself living in our home in Dhaka. Rumors of rape abounded. Finally, on April 10, with great reluctance, Ed and I sent our wives and Lyndi over to West Pakistan. It was an excruciating farewell. We had no assurance what the future held for us. West Pakistan was the only real choice because of visa restrictions. If they had gone further afield, they would not have been allowed back into the country.

As has always been our experience, our mission leadership was completely supportive of our decisions made on the local level. Never did they second-guess us. In our greatest moment of trial and uncertainty, we so appreciated their backing and constant prayers.

Thus began a most difficult two months. Ed and I had a Bengali houseboy whose breadth of culinary expertise besides curries was limited to Texas Hash and Chocolate Pudding Cake. I have never eaten the hash from Texas since 1971!

Within a few weeks we heard the military was ready to move out and secure the countryside. We knew that meant killings, burning of houses, looting, and rape. Jim McKinley was greatly concerned about some of his Southern Baptist missionaries in the North, directly in the path of this operation. Soon after the soldiers left Dhaka, Jim, who is a few years older than myself, but in great shape physically, announced he was going to make the one hundred mile trip to Faridpur. I volunteered to accompany him. He looked at my less then "great shape" and assured me it was going to be a rough trip. I reiterated my desire, especially in light of the fact that none of us were happy for Jim to make the trip on his own into such an unknown set of circumstances.

Leaving early in the morning we drove over fifty miles to the bank of the mighty Brahmaputra River which is a conduit of rushing water from the Indian Himalayas to the Bay of Bengal. We left our vehicle and crossed down river for three hours on a small boat. The Bengalis on the boat were hysterically telling us of the brutality of the military who had passed through a few days earlier.

Our hearts sank as we arrived on the other side and saw that the usual bustling terminal area now looked like a ghost town. Mud foundations covered with bamboo ashes were all that was left of the several hundred shops that once provided "curry and rice on the run" for the hurrying travelers. The few dazed survivors used what remaining energy they had to tell us how the navy had come in close and indiscriminately shelled their village. They pointed out dogs who were even then engaged in a barbaric feast of human flesh.

Divine Threads Within A Human Tapestry

We still had twenty miles ahead of us. A cycle rickshaw appeared with a passenger who paid his fare and left. A soldier quickly came and stole the money. The Bengali driver was exhausted and distraught. Jim told him he would give him our fare plus the stolen money if he would take us into Faridpur. Agreed, but one problem. He had no energy to pedal his three-wheeled vehicle plus two Americans. So Jim took over with the driver and me in the seat. Straight away our rickshaw went over the edge of the embankment, while three humans jumped in all directions!

No problem. With Jim's tenacity, he soon learned how to keep the rickshaw on the road. When he became tired, we would get out and push uphill and ride downhill. After some distance we found other rickshaws with fresh drivers who took us on into the city.

Along the way, on both sides of the road, we observed that seventy-five percent of all the houses had been burned by the military. It was all so senseless and brutal. They had made a powerful statement of intimidation. "Mess with us and this will be your fate!"

Reaching the Baptist compound, we were so relieved to find the Rythers and Thurmans safe. They had endured a frightening time with a mortar shell landing near their homes. One unoccupied home had bullet holes in it. Another building had been burned. But they were well and ever so grateful to see us.

Early the next morning we began our return journey to Dhaka with the Rythers accompanying us. At one point we had to walk ten miles in the blazing sun of the hottest month of the year. Amazingly, our vehicle was across the river where we had left it. While driving back in the dark, suddenly a soldier jumped in front of us with his rifle pointed at the front seat. Jim skillfully slammed on his brakes and jumped out so the soldier could see we had white faces. We survived. Few are the missionaries like Jim McKinley, who so consistently and selflessly demonstrate love and commitment to the people of their calling for over three decades. I salute him, Betty, his gracious, self-effacing wife, and their four brave children. His full story is told in his book, *Death to Life: Bangladesh.*

By June, life had settled into a routine. One went on with the rituals of existence knowing that, at any moment, grenades could be thrown by the Bengali resistance or a neighbor could be taken away by West Pakistani forces, never to be seen again. Our banker friend down the street requested us to hide his family in our home for a time. This we were glad to do. The people across the street had fled to a distant village. I tried to disable their car so the soldiers could not steal it. One day they brought a mechanic who installed the part I had removed. Gleefully, they drove off, convinced they were only partaking of the spoils of war, to which they were entitled.

Though Ed Welch is my best male friend, he is still no substitute for Julie. We gave the green light to our wives to start pushing for the necessary permission to return to Dhaka. That would include Bill and Anne Barnett as well. After some hassles with the authorities in West Pakistan, they were allowed to join us in June. Ed Welch flew over to have a vacation with Irene before their return.

So now our mission had six of us adults in the country. Lyndi was the only child, so got lots of attention. She was a real trooper. During the conflict, George Verwer came to visit us. One evening he was insistent on going out and discreetly dropping tracts from the slightly open car door. Just as he and I left, Lyndi looked pensively at her mother and said, "Will Daddy ever come back?" Well, we made it, but since it rained that night, I'm sure the tracts got drowned along the roadside. Anyhow, George felt good about the foray.

Another memorable time was when Jim McKinley and I went to the American Consulate to give a report on conditions in the small town where Jim and his family were living when the crackdown first occurred. The room was full of suited American officials, including the number two man to the ambassador who had flown over from West Pakistan. Jim gave a passionate rebuke of the Pakistani military excesses against helpless civilians. He was there in Feni with his wife and four small children the day the air force bombed and strafed the town. I was very proud of Jim and his defense of the defenseless.

On another occasion Julie and I took Lyndi over to the McKinleys for supper and to watch the President give a television speech from West Pakistan. Just at dusk, Betty went to bring the children from outside where they had been playing. They walked in and immediately a massive shoot-out began. Right outside the gate, freedom fighters had engaged the soldiers at a roadblock. Bullets were flying everywhere, including two which hit the house. All of us were flat on the floor. I looked over at Lyndi and said, "This is just like the Wild West!"

On television the President's voice continued to drone on, "Let me assure you, everything is normal in East Pakistan." And perhaps he was right. Normality had deteriorated to the point of insanity. When the shooting stopped, Jim went out into the yard and found three young men, probably guerrillas, hiding behind the wall. He politely urged them to leave.

Relief Ministry

My most memorable exploit occurred when I was able to obtain a large sum of money from a foreign relief agency. The overnight steamer ride to Barisal was uneventful. I made contact with the Anglicans who provided me with a small boat and boatman who would slowly paddle me through the rice fields out to a rural area where the people were on the verge of starvation.

As we came through the rice fields we saw a village which had been torched by the soldiers. Almost every house had been burned to the ground. The people were beside themselves with grief and anger. How they appreciated a white face who showed empathy to them in their moment of great peril and suffering.

Further down the canal, I arrived at the mission outpost. The Christians were hungry and distressed. They assured me the gift would assist them in buying rice for themselves and well as for their Hindu and Muslim neighbors. Shared adversity helps bring down walls of prejudice.

On the return journey the boatman asked me if I would like to visit a freedom fighters' "hospital." I knew there was risk involved as such a facility could be strafed or bombed from the air. But, my sense of solidarity with the people was as important as my personal safety. I would not be willing to take up arms to join them in their legitimate struggle, but I would do everything possible for them short of shooting their enemies. To me, their cause was every bit as moral and right as was our American war of independence in the 1700's.

Why should they not be allowed to throw off the shackles of colonialistic oppression and gain their freedom?

The sun had just slipped beneath the horizon as we nudged our boat into the mud that surrounded a small island. A bamboo hut protruded above the rice fields. So this was a hospital? In actuality, it was an abandoned Hindu home. The ten million Hindus of Bangladesh had become a specific target of the Pakistani military which suspected them of loyalty to India. In fear, millions of Hindus had fled over the border to Calcutta, leaving behind their homes and farmland.

Several armed young men ran over to our boat, anxious to know if we were friend or foe. Satisfied that we posed no threat to them, they suggested we talk to a freedom fighter who was being "treated" in the hospital. A few minutes later an extremely handsome youth hobbled out on one foot to greet us. His story saddened, and at the same time, deeply challenged me.

Abdul was a student at the prestigious University of Dhaka when the war broke out. He fled to India where he was trained and armed by the Hindu military who had a keen desire to see united Muslim Pakistan disintegrate into disarray. Soon Abdul was back in this very area fighting the Pakistan military with a hit and run strategy. During one of the operations he took a bullet in the leg, which led to its amputation above the knee. He was indeed fortunate even to be alive.

Abdul was such a gracious and polite 20-year-old young man. My query went like this, "Abdul, you had everything going for you. You were studying in the best university in the land. You come from a good family. Why did you not just go to your village home and lie low for some time? Why did you risk everything and end up like this, a cripple for life?"

With tremendous sincerity, he looked at me and said, "Oh, it has not been a sacrifice. It is an honor and privilege to fight for the liberation of my people. I gladly will give, not just my leg, but also my life that we might be free. If Allah allows, I will once again join the battle"

Such dedication to earthly goals! What does that say to me as a Christian? I protect and pamper the flesh. I seem ready to sacrifice so little. And yet I have a cause so much greater than the overthrow of a political system. My spiritual convictions put me into a battle with eternal consequences. Heaven and hell are at stake. But how forcefully has it all affected me? Abdul's words burned into me. I have never been able to forget or discard them.

On the overnight steamer trip back to Dhaka, we were suddenly fired upon from the nearby riverbank. Screams pierced the night air as people on the open deck frantically sought to protect themselves. Those of us in cabins immediately went to the dining area in the middle of the boat. There we lay flat on the floor and prayed, some to Jesus, some to Allah, and some to one of their millions of Hindu gods. The soldiers on the steamer fired back aimlessly toward the shore. And the captain kept us going full steam ahead. After five minutes, we were out of range and safely on our way to Dhaka. Home never looked so good!

Chapter 8

Civil War: The End

By September of 1971, I was emotionally and physically wearing down. It had been over a year since I had had a break. The easiest alternative was to go to Cox's Bazar, a beach at the very southern tip of the country. Accommodations would be sparse, but at least it would be an opportunity to break the routine of listening *ad infinitum* to the Bengalis' stories of sorrow.

At least so I thought. Upon arrival the Bengalis swarmed us. Seeing our white faces, they knew they had someone who cared. Even though the people were upset with American Government policy that had "tilted" toward West Pakistan, they knew the media and many American citizens supported their cause. So, once again, we were caught in a situation that demanded an outpouring of emotional empathy, a demand that I had no reserves to meet. The stories of mass killings, burning of homes, looting, and rape of young, pretty Bengali virgins was creating a serious overload on my nervous system. We had no desire to go out onto the beach because stories were told of bodies buried there.

I well remember the moment in our third rate hotel room when I was totally overwhelmed. Tension assailed every nerve-ending of my body. I felt this was the end. I could not go on. No more to give. I was an Elijah sitting under the juniper tree. Desolate, forsaken, whipped down. I was finished. It was all over.

But there was God, and there was Julie. Well, I admit, God seemed quite remote, while Julie was extremely close and intimate.

First, God. One thing I have learned over the years is that while the Lord may be hidden within the shadows of life, He is never absent. Call it blind faith if you will. But I so appreciate the latter verses of chapter eight of Romans where the believer is assured that absolutely nothing is able to separate him (or her) from the love of Christ. The disciples in the Garden of Gethsemane may have "forsaken and fled." But from the Lord's side, we are assured He will *never* leave nor forsake us, in whatever moment of peril or depression we may find ourselves. There is always, always a presence of divinity working in us and alongside us. Therefore I did not curse God for my sad plight, rather I cried to Him for release, comfort, and a renewed sense of His abiding self.

Secondly, Julie. She was just there, a precious, physical presence. In her ministry of mercy and tenderness she kept assuring me that the sun would shine yet once again. The darkness would be dispelled. Soon the genocide of East Pakistan would cease. Her words seemed hollow, but her warm embrace transmitted a love that was unconditional and permanent. I enfolded myself in her arms and there found a vicarious strength that enabled me not to go down for the full count.

We got on a dilapidated bus for the 90 mile trip north to Chittagong. I just sat in a daze, looking out the window, wondering if my wife and six-year-old daughter were destined to have such a broken down husband and dad. How could that be the will of God? Nothing made sense. Confusion. Hurt.

In Chittagong, I purchased a small bottle of tranquilizers. That, in itself, represented a defeat to my spiritual "conviction" that chemicals are not the answer to peace. They really did not help, so I threw them away. We flew to Dhaka where I went to a doctor and unloaded my burdens. After a thorough check-up he pronounced me physically in good shape and suggested a break totally away from East Pakistan

Never did I share my emotional struggles with our two missionary families. I fought to maintain a correct composure before them. Julie, along with the doctor, were my only confidants. Perhaps our colleagues were surprised to hear that we were going to fly over to West Pakistan so soon after our return from Cox's Bazar. But they never questioned me or pressured me to take them into my private space. They were, as usual, supportive and gracious. Also, we were the ones who had not been out of the turmoil. And, again, because of visas we could not leave Pakistan.

Surely, gazing upon the grandeur of the mountains surrounding Murree, along with imbibing clean, fresh, cool air would be a balm to my soul. No dead bodies to gaze upon, no horror stories to empathize with. Yes, peace has an address. Murree, Pakistan, here we come.

Sadly, it did not work out that way. Missionaries to Pakistan would sit and listen to me pour out my venom against the atrocities being committed that very moment by the Pakistani military. But within a brief time I would notice their eyes glaze over, and an attempt would be made to change the subject. After all, it was *their people* I was denouncing with such great vehemence. They felt my bias was myopic. After all, was it not treason for the East Pakistani leaders to spearhead a revolt that would cause the dismemberment of the country?

No healing. Only more anger, as well as apprehension that I would not be in East Pakistan if India joined the conflict on the side of the Bengalis. This would mean total war which, though bloody, would inevitably lead to the creation of a new nation already pre-named Bangladesh. I did not want to miss that golden moment even at the cost of the elusive peace for which I longed.

Our close friends in ICF, Merle and Gloria Inniger, invited us to accompany them for a weekend to Karachi Beach on the southern coast. We stayed in a little shack near the water's edge. The Innigers were great healing agents as they listened with insight and sensitivity to my litany of hurts. Even though Merle had a deep affinity to the West Pakistanis, still he could enter into the reality of the situation we described.

The long, basically deserted beach was also therapeutic. What fun it was to watch the huge ocean turtles paddle up on the beach and move toward the dry sand. There they used their back legs to bore a deep hole into which they dropped their eggs. Afterwards they filled in the hole to protect the eggs from predators. As they ambled back toward the ocean, we got on their backs and enjoyed a short ride into the water.

Another "crisis moment" occurred as I took an inner-tube out onto the massive waves. It took all my strength to remain seated in the tube as the waves threw me at will in all directions. Frequently, I ended upside down. Suddenly, I found myself laughing loudly in abandoned ecstasy, laughing as I had not done in a year. My emotions were being released through the agency of the crashing waves of the ocean. How good it felt.

There were still difficult days of stress to be encountered. But this began an incremental healing process that moved me toward 1974, by which time the nervous tension problem had basically been resolved. I still have an excessive number of headaches and back pains that are triggered by stress, but these problems are minuscule compared to the dark night of the soul which I had endured for 14 years.

From Karachi we flew back to Dhaka. We had been able to return before the inevitable war broke loose. India was moving its troops to the borders of both East and West Pakistan. Rhetoric on both sides was inflammatory. India was poised to invade momentarily and free the Bengali people. We dreaded the warfare, but greatly anticipated our liberation.

Beginning of the End

December 3, 1971. Indira Ghandi, the Prime Minister of India, came on All India Radio at 11 PM and announced a declaration of war against Pakistan. Julie and I listened to the short wave broadcast. Turning off the radio, with a sign of resignation, I looked at Julie and said, "Okay, that is it, there will be bombs falling on Dhaka tonight. Let us decide how we will handle it." It did not take too long to run through the options. An inner hallway measuring 5' by 3' offered the best protection from flying glass and bomb shrapnel.

Staying with us were New Zealand Baptist Missionary Society friends Stuart and Janet Avery and their four children, who had just come from boarding school in Murree, West Pakistan. The school closed because of the imminent war. Ojit, our faithful houseboy, and his family plus one of the employees in the Bible Correspondence

School added to our group, making a total of 18 people for whom I felt responsible. The Avery kids were from ages four to twelve, while Lyndi was six.

3 AM. Sirens. The first blast was totally deafening, causing the whole house to shudder. In quick succession the bombs kept falling, seemingly without end. I ran though the house, telling everyone to quickly join us in our "shelter." As we crushed together, sitting on the floor, all of us adults sought to be as cheerful as possible. We knew the children were intently watching us and would incorporate our reactions into their emotional responses. By God's grace, from that initial moment right through the next 13 days of horror, each of the 18 persons living with us remained amazingly composed. Not one case of hysteria or psychosomatic problems. The Lord was indeed gracious to all of us.

During bombing pauses Stuart and I would go up to the flat cement roof of our house and watch the dog fights between the Pakistani and Indian fighter planes. It was sad to see many planes crash. Only a few parachutes floated downward from disabled aircraft. Within three days the Pakistan Air Force was destroyed. Indian bomber planes had free run of the air space over Dhaka. However, they had to dodge a sky full of anti-aircraft fire. Shrapnel fell as rain. Once a blazing hot piece of steel came pummeling down landing a few feet from where I was standing.

Dhaka International Airport was a close two miles from us. The runway was a key target of the bombers. Though the Indians were able to damage it, they never put it out of commission. Frequently we would hear the wailing of the air raid sirens. Within five minutes the planes would appear in the sky. Bomb blasts coupled with the noise of the anti-aircraft guns were almost overwhelming. It was particularly difficult in the solid blackness of night. A total blackout was rigidly enforced. We got around that by putting heavy blankets on the windows of one room which enabled us to keep a small light on. To the delight of the children, they had our complete attention for hours on end while we all played a variety of games.

Masking tape was applied in a crisscross design on the windows, which would lessen the danger of flying glass if they were shattered. During short reprieves from the curfew, we were able to get adequate food from the market because merchants also rushed there to sell what they could. Our water supply never failed us though electricity was erratic.

With my usual journalistic flair, one afternoon I suggested to the Averys that we go check out the airport. Loading up the car, we drove around the perimeter of the runway. A number of bombs had fallen short of their target and one had landed on an orphanage, killing a number of children. We saw one totally exposed, unexploded bomb lying in a small lane. In another area we saw deep craters right beside bamboo houses. As we stood talking to the people, the sirens went off. We knew we had five minutes to make our getaway from the airport. Seldom have I driven that fast and furious.

On another occasion I drove over to the small Southern Baptist compound where 45 people were taking shelter. Jim McKinley was showing his usual amazing composure and strong faith in the Lord. Suddenly, the sirens went off and most everyone took shelter. But Jim and I went up on the roof and saw what I shall never forget. The Indian planes were strafing close to the McKinley home. They were flying so low that I could see the pilots' faces. We were to meet those same air force officers a few days later.

Another Evacuation

On December 6 there was supposed to be an arranged truce for a few hours that would allow all the foreigners to be evacuated on US Air Force planes. Later we learned that Julie's cousin, a colonel in the Strategic Air Command, had courageously volunteered to fly in one of the planes so he could "rescue his cousin and her family." Little did he know that we had no intention to leave our people. The planes flew high over the city, but the shooting never stopped, so they returned to their base in Thailand.

The American consulate was strongly urging all foreigners to leave. Everyone was supposed to take one suitcase and stay each day at the Intercontinental Hotel. Evacuation could take place at any moment. I highly commend the consulate officials for all of their zeal and compassion.

Finally, on December 12, the American C-130's made it to Dhaka. They circled the city numerous times, and then flew low over the runway, seeking to evaluate if they could make a safe landing. An awesome silence prevailed as we watched this drama from our roof. Great puffs of dust rose up into the blue sky when the tires finally touched the tarmac. Engines never stopped. Within minutes they were airborne again. As I watched the small dots disappear over the horizon, I felt lonely, very lonely. "Oh God, what if I have made a terrible mistake in having us all remain behind?" Finality. Soul-searing finality. Options closed. The sacredness of the quiet moment was broken by yet another air-raid siren and resumed bombing.

Only twelve foreign children remained in Dhaka. Lyndi, the four Avery children, and seven Southern Baptist MK's. What courageous kids! They ministered deeply to all of us parents.

After December 12, Hotel Intercontinental was declared a Red Cross neutral area that would not be shelled by either side. All remaining foreigners were urged to take up residence there. Every indication was that soon house to house fighting would be taking place. The Indian soldiers had reached the outskirts of the city and were poised to attack. All through our neighborhood, trenches were being hastily dug. The Pakistani commander of Dhaka had said he would "let the city be reduced to rubble" before he would agree to surrender. Bad news!

Thousands of leaflets floated down from Indian planes. They ordered all foreigners to leave and urged Pakistani forces to surrender. If they did, they would be guaranteed safety. Any thought of our leaving was a joke. Mortar shells from the Indian ground troops were starting to fly in from the suburbs. There would be no safe haven anywhere. The safest place was in our home, praying, and waiting.

There were 200,000 civilians and 40,000 Pakistani soldiers left in Dhaka. No one felt the Pakistanis could win, but all indicators pointed to a blood bath prior to a forced surrender. Would some of that blood include that of a missionary remnant which was scattered in several areas of the city? A heavy pall of gloom settled over Dhaka.

Throughout the afternoon of the 15th a stillness reigned. No bombing sorties, no mortar shells. Could it be that a surrender was being negotiated? Was it too much to hope for?

Birth

December 16, 1971. We first received the news through the Far East Broadcasting Corporation's short-wave English newscast from Manila, Philippines. They announced that the war was over. Pakistan had capitulated. With shouts of "Joy Bangla" ("Victory to Bengal") we went up on our roof and reinstalled our Bangladesh flag. Soon hordes of people were shouting and hugging one another. A new nation was born. At 5:01 PM the official surrender was signed.

My "Birth Announcement" of the nation of Bangladesh was written as follows:

March 25, 1971 to December 16, 1971. A nine month full-term waiting period which included fourteen days of agonizing labor followed by the bloody Cesarean birth of the world's eighth largest nation.

Name: Bangladesh

Size: 75 million people

Disposition: Extremely jubilant

Prognosis: Democratic, socialistic, and secularistic.

How good the fresh air of freedom felt, blowing hard against my innermost being! "Free at last, free at last, Praise God, we are free at last."

Chapter 9

A New Start

On the morning of December 17, I went to the modest home of the Sheikh where his wife was staying. She had been kept under house arrest for the nine months of the civil war. Along with journalists, I interviewed this rather simple village woman who, by a quirk of history, was married to one of the most famous men in the world. She emotionally pleaded with newsmen to put pressure on West Pakistani authorities to release her husband from prison. She, like us, knew that in a moment of anger and frustration, anyone, from jailer to President, could have the Sheikh dispatched to eternity. It was a tenuous and uncertain moment for the Sheikh, his family, and the newborn country of Bangladesh. The nation for which he was willing to die desperately needed his charismatic leadership. We were living in a vacuum superintended by the Indian military. No one wanted the Hindu soldiers to be the new colonial power of Bangladesh. The sooner they withdrew the better it would be for everyone.

That same morning we and the Avery family drove to the airport to see what damage had been done there. A helicopter had just landed from Calcutta with a number of Indian pilots who had bombed and strafed the city. They invited us into their helicopter and lifted it barely off the ground. A great treat for the kids! Several pilots who had shot up the presidential palace requested us to drive them into the city to see the fruit of their dangerous mission. This we did, which also allowed us to have a "tour' of the bombed out palace. It was sad to see all the destruction.

Next on the agenda was a trip 40 miles out of the city to Manikganj, the village where we had spent our first term. Much to my relief, I found that Ed and Irene Welch, along with Bill and Anne Barnett, were safe and sane. There had been no problem in Manikganj. Bill, with his Scottish twinkle, complained, "Hey, we missed all the fun!" It was a privilege to have these two quality couples ministering with us. The Welches remained in Bangladesh for 12 years and the Barnetts served for 20 years. Both families are still with SIM in their respective home offices.

On December 18, I noticed a long line of people making their way out to the fields behind our home. Soon word came that scores of bodies had been dumped in the brick fields about a mile distant. I left the house and made the pilgrimage out to the area. How shocking to gaze down from an elevated mound of dirt and see the blindfolded, tied up, decaying corpses of some of the intellectual elite of Dhaka. Vultures had moved in and commenced their feast.

We had heard that collaborators had been moving around Dhaka in vans during the curfew hours on December 14 and 15. Now I understood what their gruesome task had been. They picked up doctors, bankers, professors, and businessmen, drove them to the brick field, and shot them. Even today it is still hard to imagine what diabolic motivation prompted them to engage in such acts of barbarism during the last dying moments of East Pakistan. How can anyone help but believe in the depraved nature of man?

One last illustration. Many of the Pakistani soldiers were sexual brutes. Young Bengali girls were taken into the military camps and raped repeatedly by the men. Forced abortions were performed on those who became pregnant. There were stories of girls being kept in the nude in front line trenches so they would not escape. After the war, I visited a Christian compound which had been taken over by the military. Draped over wooden crossbars hung the sheared long hair of the girls who had been imprisoned as sex slaves. With shorn head they would be unable to use their hair to commit suicide by hanging themselves.

Unfortunately, these happenings created a perverse sort of notoriety. Many relief workers came from Western countries and specifically wanted to help these young ladies with financial assistance, jobs, or even to facilitate the adoption of any unwanted babies. It all smacked of a low-grade sensationalism which could be used for fund-raising purposes. In reality, most of the girls were accepted back into parental homes with a realization that they were victims of coercion.

The good news came on January 8. Sheikh Mujibur Rahman had been released from prison in West Pakistan and was flying back to Dhaka via London. Bengalis were absolutely ecstatic. Grandiose preparations were made for his return. The immense race course would be the venue of his first statement to his newly-birthed nation.

What a day January 10 was! Julie, Lyndi, and Marian Olson decided to avoid the massive crowd and go to the roof of Hotel Intercontinental for an excellent view of the procession route as well as the race course. That was fine for them, but Cal Olson and I wanted to be more a part of the action. With cameras around our necks and white skin prominently displayed, we walked down the street from the hotel to the race course, acknowledging the cheers and laughter of the waiting thousands, prior to the arrival of the Sheikh's entourage. When we got to the bottom of the stairs leading up to the dais from which the Sheikh would address an ocean of brown faces, we paused. But not for long. Up we went and over to one side to await our hero's arrival.

An hour later, an emaciated Sheikh, dressed immaculately in his trademark Awami League jacket, was pushed through the adoring crowds and up onto the platform. He then sat on the stage, put his head in his hands and wept. A most moving moment. I, at times, was just a few feet from this great statesman. He then stood before the microphone, told his prison story, commiserated with the sorrowing, and exhorted everyone to get on with the task of nation-building. He was a spellbinding orator. Never in the history of Dhaka had there been such a day.

A week later, along with others, I interviewed the Sheikh in the garden of his home. All of the media had been saying that one million Bengalis had been killed during the civil war. On that warm afternoon, I heard from the Sheikh's own lips that three million of his countrymen had been murdered in the genocide of Bangladesh. That struck me as pure exaggeration as that would require 12,000 persons to have been killed each day. Perhaps 500,000 total would be a more accurate estimate. No one will ever know, because precise counting does not occur in Bangladesh.

The flood gates opened to the country. In came relief and development agencies from around the world. I became a somewhat popular commodity as a person to see, one who has the inside story of the "rape of Bangladesh." (Round 1) the hurricane. (Round 2) the civil war. When would all of this tragedy end? I was exhausted.

A letter came to me from Stanley Mooneyham, director of World Vision, asking me to assist in getting their program established. After prayer for guidance, I decided to focus my energies on assisting this interdenominational Christian organization. I was consignee for all of their goods, along with being an advisor to their local director. Through this means, I felt I was having some specific part in the rehabilitation of a wounded nation.

Some interesting Christians showed up during those days. One way-out evangelist from America called me one day and assured me he was "God's parachutist." That is, in times of tragedy when hearts are restless, he chutes up and drops in with a message of peace and salvation that people just cannot refuse. It was important for him to meet with all the local leaders and plan for a massive crusade at the race course. I assured him I was washed out and just did not possess the energy he had for such a huge undertaking.

Not to be put off, he asked if I ate lunch each day. Not a bad line. I fell for it and said that was my usual custom. Quick as a flash, he pulled in the line with me on the hook. The next day found me sitting with him and other "fish" he had caught, eating lunch at the, by now, famous Hotel Intercontinental. What a pitch he gave, complete with photos of the thousands who had attended his meetings in Muslim Indonesia. "Now is God's hour for Bangladesh," he assured us as his accompanying media man took our pictures from various angles.

It all seemed so artificial and sub-Christian. We were polite, but non-committal. In subsequent days he pushed on every door he could. No response. After a week of draining his expense account, he and his PR friend left Bangladesh, exclaiming, "God can do nothing in this land because of the lack of faith and commitment of the Christians." So be it.

A positive experience was the visit of Bob Pierce, founder of World Vision, and at the time he visited Bangladesh, president of Samaritan's Purse. He graciously invited all of the Dhaka missionaries to a lovely meal and time of sharing. What a balm for our weary hearts as we shared intimate thoughts with one another. Bob's absolute candor about his failures as a husband and father first shocked us and then caused us to appreciate him as a vulnerable pilgrim. Somehow our individual inadequacies came into better and more manageable perspective as we listened to this man of God openly confess his sins and then tell of his appropriation of grace. How different he was from so many suave, highly polished, "Hi, how are you, sooo good to see you," Christian leaders.

And so, a turbulent era in the Parshalls' lives drew to a close.

In early 1972, I had the joy of attending our mission's International Conference in Tehran, Iran. On the way, I stopped in Kabul, Afghanistan, for a week. I had the privilege of speaking to the tentmakers there on a Wednesday evening just prior to their moving into their new church. This was the same edifice that was bulldozed to the ground by Muslim fanatics a few weeks later. I have always been grateful for my visits to those two countries in light of subsequent events that happened there.

Our year of home service was coming up in June of 1972. There was no way I was agreeable to take another heavy deputation tour. Early in that year I had decided to try to pursue my growing interest in further academic study. But who would take a chance on me for graduate work in light of my unaccredited B.A. degree from Tennessee Temple College?

In Dhaka I was able to take the Graduate Records Exam. My total score was poor. So what did I have to commend myself intellectually? Actually, nothing. I sent in applications to only two grad schools. Wheaton said I was not up to their standard and to apply elsewhere. Thanks a lot! I have had a lot of fun with those guys as I later got an M.A. there and have taught in their grad school. Also, I was offered part-time faculty status in connection with a position at the Wheaton Graham Center. Having said all that (I feel better now), I really do not blame them for pulling up the bridge over the moat. That made good academic sense. They followed the letter of the law.

But I was in pursuit of *grace.* Would not some merciful admissions committee give me a chance? Dr. Herbert Kane was sitting on one such committee at Trinity Evangelical Divinity School when my papers were brought up for discussion. Herb tells of the next critical moments in his unpublished autobiography. He relates how he gently coerced the group to go out on a limb and see if this unknown missionary from Bangladesh could make the grade at TEDS. "Let's put him on probation and see what happens." *Thank you, Lord.!* He later became my mentor and close friend.

Family Conversion

How naïve it was to even consider attending an expensive seminary without the benefit of savings, scholarships, or a promise of financial assistance. But the Lord had a dramatic solution to that problem. Soon after arrival in the States, we drove down to Miami to spend a few weeks with my relatives.

The first afternoon, Jimmy, my brother, came over to Mom and Dad's home to see us. That in itself was most unusual, but the shocker was when he cordially invited us over to his home to spend the night. I had never spent an overnight in Jimmy's home. What new thing was this! Besides, he was downright friendly. Strange indeed.

Later that evening, Jimmy dropped the bombshell. "I have become a Christian." Five little words, but totally revolutionary in impact. After 17 arduous years of prayer, could I be hearing right? And then a faithless thought bombarded me. What kind of "Christian?" Within the hundreds of interpretive choices, had my brother really found the straight and narrow path that alone leads to eternal life?

Anxiety, and then ecstatic relief. Jimmy's Baptist foreman who was working for him in his ornamental iron shop had been a quiet, consistent witness for Christ. This, coupled with memories of my testimony, along with a certain amount of despair because two of his teen-age children were in a drug rehabilitation program, made him more sensitive to the claims of the Lord on his life. He stood before me a two-month-old newborn in the faith.

Wow! Really? A Christian. What rejoicing together. Later, I led his wife, Shirley, to Christ. Within a few weeks I was able to point his three children to the Savior. Some months later Jimmy led Dad to a profession of faith and then he and I witnessed to Mom, bringing her to confess Jesus as Redeemer. A Grand Slam. How good it has been to see them grow in the Lord. Not without real struggles and occasional setbacks, but what a tremendous encouragement to see God's hand at work within my family.

Now, back to the morning after that memorable night. Jimmy went to the bank, returned home, and thrust a wad of bills into my hand. "If I am to be a Christian, then I want to be one in totality. I am going to tithe corporation profits to you and your ministry. Here is the first installment of 525 dollars." I was overwhelmed. Here is this alienated brother who once called me a "great con-man" because of my ability to raise money for exotic trips abroad. Now he, without any suggestion from me, is starting down a path that would pay for my M.A. at Trinity and funnel thousands of dollars into our Bangladesh evangelistic outreach. Such was the work of God's grace in one man's heart.

This alienated brother became an intimate friend. That summer we enjoyed an outing in his deep sea fishing boat as well as a ride in his own plane, which he piloted. It is interesting to note his well-off financial condition did not last. Jimmy has had innumerable financial reverses ever since he became a believer. So much for the "prosperity doctrine" that some unrealistic saints propagate. If my brother, as a new Christian, had fallen for that line, he probably would have walked away from Christianity when the hard times came. His absolute steadfastness to his Lord and to his family has been a model to me. Of course, his tenaciously loyal wife, Shirley, deserves most of the credit for anything he has accomplished in life. How fortunate Jimmy and I are to have the wives we have.

Further Education

Our eleven months at Trinity were both mind and heart stretching. Early on, I took a speed reading course that was academic salvation to me. Thousands of pages had to be read and lightly assimilated. Without that course, I would have bogged down and, at minimum, have become an absentee husband/father. Writing the many assigned papers seemed to just come naturally. Julie assisted me with the research and did all of my typing. It was fun to work as a team, which is what we have enjoyed doing all our married life.

An amazing metamorphosis took place as I came into the scholastic arena of life. Somehow it all ignited and became challenging and fun. I make absolutely no claim to being an intellectual. I just do not think or comprehend like a person trained in the classics, history, or philosophy. Also, my memory is far from the photographic variety. But I became a tenacious plodder, with focus. The discipline of Missiology excited me and just seemed so practically beneficial to all I was doing in life. The result was that my grades on the graduate degree level turned out very well. Truly, the Lord has been gracious and helpful to me in my academic pursuits.

Out of that year came an M.A. in Missiology and a thesis which was later published in India under the title, *The Fortress and the Fire*. There were no royalties for this book. All subsequent royalties for my writings and speaking have been funneled into our "ministry funds" which are controlled by SIM. I have strong convictions against the personal use of any such money gained while in the service of Christ.

Repeatedly, while at Trinity, I was given reading assignments of books which were authored by professors who were teaching at Fuller Seminary's School of World Mission. This exposure to the principles of cross-cultural evangelism done in a contextual mode formed the foundation for what our team would be doing in Bangladesh in the next few years. Another key happening of that year was the Lord speaking to David Coffey, a fellow Trinity student, about returning to Bangladesh where he had been as a youth. His parents had worked there in secular employment. David then recruited Paul Thomas, and Ed Wheeler. All married gifted women and thus we gained three unique couples for Bangladesh ministry, five individuals among them with Trinity degrees and the other, Karin Thomas, a medical doctor.

November, 1973. Back to the land of our calling. The Sheikh was presiding as Prime Minister while the country was in a downward spiral. His paranoia seemed to increase as poverty stalked the nation. All government employees were being made to join his political party. Unrest spread. Love for the Sheikh was quickly turning to raw hatred.

An Encounter with the President

One day the phone rang and I found myself talking to Cal Olson. "Phil, I hear you are looking for a new office for your Bible Correspondence School. How would you like to rent the personal home of the President of Bangladesh for your school?" I really could not believe what I was hearing. Everyone knew the President, who held this largely ceremonial post under the Prime Minister, was living in the downtown palace. But his British colonial style home with a lovely garden was in a most strategic location right on the main road to the airport.

"Cal, you have got to be kidding. This Muslim President would never allow his private home to be filled with Bibles and correspondence lessons!" Cal gently moved me from disbelief to skeptical faith. I knew Cal was on an inside track because he rented another of the President's houses in the city. Out of that had developed an amazingly close relationship between a Muslim President of the world's eighth most populous country and a Pentecostal missionary!

The next day Cal and I, in his old Volkswagen, drove through the gates of the palace while guards stood at attention and saluted. We were escorted down a long hall and into a huge reception room. A short time later the eight foot high doors opened and in walked the 5'2" President. He graciously chatted with us while a hurricane battered the city outside the ostentatious confines of the palace.

While we ate delicious Bengali sweets and sipped milky tea, the President made his offer. We could occupy the bottom floor of his home, except for his book-lined office. I could even use that room, except for the times the President would be there occupying the top floor. This would give me access to a telephone with a golden number which always worked. No small amenity in a city of inadequate phones.

The large garden and circular driveway were thrown in with the deal. I held my breath as the President looked at me with his piercing eyes and announced the ridiculously low monthly rental. Seeking not to disclose my incredulity, I decided to go for broke. "Mr. President, could we have your kind permission to put a *Bangladesh Bible Correspondence School* sign in Bengali and English on the front gate?"

Without missing a beat, he said, "Yes, just be sure it is an attractive sign." I assured him it would be.

We set a date for the signing of the lease and then went to look at the inside of our new Correspondence School. It was absolutely perfect for our needs. Some days later several rented, dilapidated trucks rolled into the driveway, bringing steel cabinets, tables, chairs, and thousands of Bible lessons. Certainly this was a unique happening in the history of the world's Muslim Presidents and their personal homes.

For the next five years we thoroughly enjoyed our special relationship with the President. The first year we were invited, along with Cal and Marian Olson, to the Independence Day celebrations held in the palace gardens. Probably we were the only white-faced, non-diplomats present. The President graciously introduced us to the Sheikh. Oh, the interesting life of a missionary!

Soon the mystery of the cheap rent was solved. Against the Sheikh's desire, the President resigned. He then became a roving ambassador for Bangladesh with cabinet status. He and his family moved to Geneva, Switzerland. The President knew this move was forthcoming. He had wanted his home to be in good hands, even at a low rent. We were the beneficiaries of his concern.

Twice a year the President and family would return to Dhaka and stay in the upstairs of his home. It was interesting to see the various cabinet ministers drive through our Correspondence School gates and then meet the President in "our" office. Whenever he was home, armed soldiers stood a 24 hour guard at the entrance. This somewhat dampened the courage of our students in their desire to visit us. But the President's times in Dhaka were brief.

He and I became friends, but never as intimate as he and Cal Olson. One day I was sitting on the wide verandah and writing up a strategy to reach Bangladesh Muslims for Christ. The President walked up and said, "Mr. Parshall, what are you doing? Are you writing poetry?"

Meekly, I muttered, "Yes, sort of." He then took my hand in good Eastern fashion, and led me into the office. After ordering tea and sweets from his ever-present servant, he settled back on the couch and in a pensive mood, asked me a startling question.

"Mr. Parshall, are you a man of God like my good friend, Mr. Olson?"

Where could I take that? Cal is a walking text out of context. His body is on earth, but his serene composure puts him within the heavenlies. At one point Cal and his wife, Marian, spent six weeks in our home. From close range, I could see how Christ totally dominated his thoughts, speech, extended periods of prayer, and intensive times of fasting. To the president, Cal modeled mystical Christianity at its apex.

And so the esteemed Muslim cabinet minister just sat there and looked deep into my soul. He waited. I waited. Finally, with some hesitation, I did what every good Baptist would do. I assured the President that Cal and I believed the same Bible and were in the same fraternity of worldwide believers. He was unmoved. I was embarrassed because I knew I was out of my league when being compared to "Saint Cal."

His eyes became as a laser beam piercing my armor of cognitive orthodoxy. "Actually," he began, as he slowly measured his words, "Actually, Mr. Parshall, you remind me more of an American diplomat than you do a man of God like Mr. Olson."

Incoherence. I just verbally rambled for a while and finally excused myself. I needed time to reflect and digest the impact of those hurting words. My desire: To so live out my faith that Muslims would recognize me as having a spiritual dynamic that would draw them to the Savior. The reality, at least to the President: I was articulate, informed, and very American.

There is a reasonable chance I could have passed the foreign service exam. A diplomatic career would have involved a lot less hassle than being a missionary. But that was not my goal and passion of life. Yet, here I was being powerfully perceived to be a mere American diplomat.

After a great deal of soul-searching, I have sought to be, *in reality*, a man of God. Without doubt, this is an elongated process. But at least I have a new sensitivity to the issues. Out of this encounter came one of my most-quoted graphs. I drew up a comparison of the Muslim priest and the foreign missionary. Distinctions were highlighted. The unmistakable conclusion was that, to the onlooking Muslim, his priest looks more like a man of spiritual values (at least outwardly) than does the missionary. Something to ponder.

Chapter 10

Challenges

A sad, sad day. Just a letter, but such a powerfully devastating letter. In disbelief, I read of the admitted adultery of my spiritual father, Ray. Over the next few years, I learned the details of the fall of this great soul winner. It was amazing to hear how one sin of lust led to another and another. Incremental sin is insidious because it does not blast you all at once. Being propositioned by a beautiful prostitute is much easier to refuse than is a meaningful exchange of eye contact with an acquaintance of the opposite sex. But both can potentially lead to divorce and leaving the ministry, which is what happened to Ray.

Because of the importance of this issue, I want to address it in some detail. First, just the bare outlines of a few true stories that have touched my life (given with pseudonyms).

♦ Not only my father in the faith, but Julie's spiritual mentor fell as well. Abuse toward his wife led on to Paul's adultery and then to the forsaking of his commitment to the pastorate. It took a detective to reveal his "other life" which took place under the guise of an afternoon "Bible study." The woman's small kids were playing in the back yard, securely locked out of the house.

♦ Robert became extremely discouraged trying to learn a difficult language in the context of a remote town in one Asian country. Muslims would make fun of this young American as he stammered out his few memorized phrases. Conflict began to dominate family relationships. Robert fled into a world of sexual fantasy by reading the cheap paperbacks that were readily available in the market. One late night, Robert went into the bedroom and began to choke his sleeping wife to death. She awoke, screamed, and threw Robert off of her. He regained his senses and went out and wept through the night. Within a year, this family was on the way back to their homeland. By God's grace, they have held together and are following the Lord while engaged in secular work.

♦ Harvey met with me at an international leadership conference. We had been friends for many years and now he was a well-known missionary. At some point in our conversation he told of going to a pornographic movie in a European city. I asked him how that affected him. He said he left the theater, crossed the street, and went to another X-rated film. There did not seem to be much repentance connected with the telling of the story. A few years later, I heard he had left the mission field because of adultery. He then divorced his wife and remarried. One day I met his grown daughter. She, with poignant sorrow in her voice, said, "We had so many good times growing up together as a family on the mission field. But, you know, now it is as if all of those memories have been raped. There is no joy in my memory bank. I will never divorce my husband. Never could I do to my children what has been done to me and my siblings by my unfaithful father."

♦ Richard was our pastor during one of our students stints. How we admired this man of God who had achieved significant notoriety as an evangelical spokesman and author. When he fell into unfaithfulness, it was like I had personally suffered yet another blast at my faith. If these giants fall, what hope is there for the average Christian? How can these men deny all they have preached for decades? Out of deep frustration, I sat down and poured out my disgust in a long handwritten letter and sent it to Richard. In some ways it was a carnal letter. This man had failed me terribly. Now it was as if I wanted to hurt him in return. Not a very Christian attitude, I'm afraid. By return, I received Richard's personal letter which expressed repentance for his immorality. He then made a statement that continues to bother me. "I do not feel that I am any greater a sinner now, in the sight of God and man, than I was before I committed adultery." Because of the forgiving grace of our Lord, he may make it okay in the sight of God. But his reputation has been forever downgraded in the sight of man. Sorry, you cannot just go and commit adultery and not pay the consequences. David, Nathan, and Psalm 51 bear me out.

Unfortunately, I could continue for some time with this list of illustrations. This, however, is adequate to highlight the impact these failures have had on me. In some ways, they have made me a skeptic. If I know of so many who have fallen, how many more are there who have yet to be found out? A depressing thought!

Why the conundrum of man's total vulnerability to sexual temptation? Like the sudden illumination of a darkened room by the flick of a light switch, just so are male sex hormones instantaneously activated by a look, a picture, a sound, or most persistently, a thought. Relentlessly, the mind and emotions are bombarded by stimuli that manufacture sin.

Why do I say "men?" *Playboy* sells much better than *Playgirl*. Who goes to the X-rated movies? Who is the initiator in most acts of adultery? In my down moments, I have accused God of an unfair distribution of the sex drive. "Why not fifty percent for men and fifty percent for women, Lord?" There is probably not a deeply committed Christian man who has not cried out to God repeatedly for sexual purity. I do not believe that is true regarding women. Some, of course, have prayed that prayer, but more often their concern is on the emotional level of attraction to men rather than relating to raw sexual urges. But, of course, this can lead on to the same act of immorality.

And so we must take life as we find it. Satan loves our points of vulnerability. The motif of a "roaring lion going about seeking whom he may devour" is totally appropriate. He knows where to make his hit. The Christian absolutely must actively engage in this battle. Passivity will lead to defeat.

In 1970, I found myself in a nice hotel in Bangkok, Thailand, which had been arranged by the airlines as a free overnight stopover on my trip to Singapore. The porter placed my bag in the room and offered to send in a girl for five dollars. Refusing his suggestion, I went downstairs for a brief walk in a nice area of the city before supper. In the lobby the doorman gave me a card for a massage parlor which he assured me was the best in the city. In the next few minutes I was propositioned several times by beautiful Thai girls.

I quickened my pace back to my room, got on my knees and thanked God that I had not capitulated to the flesh. Not one person in Bangkok knew me. At that young age, but by the grace of God, I could have ruined myself as a husband, father, and missionary. Over the years of my travels, many other "propositions" have come and gone, but I continue to value eminently the reality of my sustained devotion to my family and my Lord. Oh, how worthwhile is the battle.

I do have some "heroes" in regard to moral integrity. The greatest of these is Robertson McQuilkin, the retired President of Columbia International University. In 1986, we in the Philippines had the privilege of having Robertson and his wife Muriel join us in the southern island of Mindanao to speak at our spiritual life conference. Several of us noted Muriel's forgetfulness. Still she was a beautiful person in every way. It was fun to watch the interplay between the McQuilkins. Obviously they were deeply in love.

Since that time in 1986, I have frequently been able to visit Robertson and Muriel in their little home in a less than desirable neighborhood of Columbia, South Carolina. Muriel went through the usual degenerative stages of Alzheimer's disease. For a time she was extremely restless, always moving things around, and trying to get out of the house. Next came incontinence. Robertson became the expert diaper changer. And now Muriel is mute and unable to walk. In mind, she is no longer in this world.

All through this extreme trial, Robertson has been the primary caregiver. He feeds, bathes, and clothes Muriel. Almost every foundation of their married life has been destroyed. Emotional and physical relationships are finished. What is left? Only steadfast love and commitment remain. And so Robertson models for me and others what true marital fidelity is all about. I guess the question that will not let me go is, "Why do some leaders fall when the temptation seems minimal while others continue to stand when 'situation ethics' would give them a go signal for an extra-marital affair?"

Thus, we are brought back to the Word of God. Biblical commands and norms in regard to morality are explicit. First Corinthians 10:13 assures us we do not have to be defeated by temptation. Like Joseph, we can always look for the door of escape. It is there. The Lord has given us free will. We can choose to turn away, or simply to capitulate to the allure of the world. I am convinced that as Christian men, we will need to continue making that choice until our last breath.

Within a one week span in 1974, 14 new missionaries joined our team in Bangladesh. A huge hassle in regard to orientation, but what a delight to have a larger team to work with. We were 27 adults from six countries and more than a quiver full of kids. Our family moved into a small two bedroom apartment just two blocks from our "Presidential" Bible Correspondence School office. Anne Barnett then capably oversaw our mission guest house, while her husband Bill became the business administrator-cum-treasurer. We as a mission were ready to launch into new depths.

More Suffering

But first we had to deal with the great famine of 1974. The following is a reflection I wrote during those horrible days. Each of these experiences actually occurred.

An Eternity of Suffering

A desperate, destitute family of four recklessly throw their bodies before an onrushing train. Their screams stretch to eternity....

The final meal of curry and rice is carefully prepared by a distraught mother of six. A generous portion of rat poison merges with the swirling mass of boiling juice. The kiss of death and then... eternity.

A frightened little boy of nine scans the garbage heap for a morsel of food. He scurries back to his dying father with a soggy crust of bread. It's too late. Too late... eternity!

Divine Threads Within A Human Tapestry

For some, eternity begins with death. For others in Bangladesh, this life seems an eternity because of relentless hunger and privation.

She was just twenty and possessed the potential of being quite attractive. The emaciated baby clutching her exposed breast was so tiny and ever so helpless. Gratefully accepting the gift of 75 cents, the hungry mother slowly walked away. Her rags of clothing were so inadequate that her bare buttocks literally screamed the message of poverty to an insensitive, onlooking world.

Home is a sidewalk. The drain is the bathroom. Two bricks are the stove. Gathered cow dung provides the fuel. A dead crow is supper for mom, dad, and three small children.

Eternity is now, and eternity is hell! Eternity is being hungry, and eternity is Bangladesh.

Thousands of poverty-stricken families continue to stream into the weary and dying capital of Bangladesh. Dhaka, once a proud center of Islamic culture, struggles for even a semblance of composure. The wail of the hungry, and the mournful call of the minaret, waft cheerlessly together across the scores of hastily constructed shantytowns. It is the Muslim month of fasting, but no man nor religion need dictate abstinence. There is no option, there is no viable alternative.

The rural scene likewise is grim. Floods have ruthlessly destroyed thousands of acres of crops. In desperation, families gather their belongings and sadly begin the trek to the nearest town or city. There they find only further misery and hurt. And... they also find eternity.

Just for a few moments, do me a favor and "sit where they sit." Let your precious father be that dying old man. Picture your daughter begging at the entrance to the Dhaka post office only half-covered by her rags. Taste that diseased crow as it is drawn out of the dung-fed flame. Contemplate the option of the onrushing train as compared to the cooked rat poison.

How, then, does your life relate to the eternity of Bangladesh?

In various ways, we sought to assist the suffering Bengalis. Once again, the Grim Reaper stalked the land of Bangladesh. We often wondered if he would ever finish his harvest and leave us alone!

Contextualization

Now to our new approach to ministry. Contextualization is a much maligned word that simply points to a context. For us, that meant presenting the biblical message of salvation in Christ in such a manner that it could maximally be understood, and hopefully accepted, by the Muslim Bengalis. It seemed to us that what little evangelism had been done among the Children of Ishmael had not been culturally sensitive to the context of Muslim thought and life. I tried to illustrate the concept by putting the incarnation into a Bangladesh setting.

I Had a Dream

There standing before me on a dusty path
in a remote village of Bangladesh
stood Jesus.
His ganji and lungi were soiled,
His brow filled with sparkling beads
of perspiration.
Hands of labor radiated a message
of dignity.
Callused feet spoke of hours behind
a plow.
His brown, golden skin communicated a
startling truth.
God had become a Bengali!

I fell upon the hot blistering earth in
awe and reverence.
His hands of love tenderly embraced me
and drew me to His breast.
His voice spoke with the tenderness
of the flow of a small rippling brook,
Yet, with the authority of the roaring Ganges,
"Come, my Bengali child,

Come and follow me."
My conquered will could only respond with
words of brokenness,
    "My Lord and My God."
Slowly rising to my feet, I found myself struggling
    for composure.
        "What new thing is this?"

My heart was as joyous as the dancing of the
    newborn lamb;
My tattered clothing seemed as regal as that of the
    wealthy land owner;
My aching limbs became as refreshed as if I had just
    bathed in the cool waters of the nearby pond;
The gnawing pangs of hunger subsided as if I
    had just eaten a most sumptuous meal of
        rice and curry
Yes, now I understand, I have just accepted
    Jesus Of Bengal
        As My Lord...
            My God.

What a great privilege to hammer out a new strategy of evangelism with such a sharp group of enthusiastic, energetic, courageous missionaries. It was entirely a team effort. Unfortunately, the credit (as well as the rather minimal criticism) has flowed in my direction. Never could I have put together such a missiological construct on my own. A few key Muslim converts, as well as each of our missionaries, were the builders. Perhaps my role could best be described as the coordinator. Later, I became the one who unveiled our methodology through my writings. But I want to clearly disassociate myself from any unilateral credit for the efforts and any results that have accrued from the new strategy.

Our evangelistic *modus operandi* has been thoroughly documented in my book *New Paths in Muslim Evangelism*. Never, to my knowledge, did anyone from any mission in Bangladesh criticize our efforts. They were extremely supportive in every way. Some joined ranks and commenced their own contextualized outreach among Muslims. Our mission's general director at that time, George Hemming, was one hundred percent behind us.

Unfortunately, many in the established Bengali Church struggled deeply with our methodology. They saw it as a compromise with Islam. The exciting thing is that, over the past 25 years, some within this body of believers have accepted the principles of contextualization and launched out to establish a number of quasi-homogeneous Muslim convert churches.

How many Muslim converts are there in Bangladesh? I do not have any specific estimates to offer in regard to statistical data. In any event, it probably would not be wise to publicize figures. What can be said is the Lord has done a real work of His liberating grace in many hearts.

Word filtered out that there would be a huge gathering of several thousand Christian leaders in Lausanne, Switzerland, July 16-25, 1974. Secretly, I longed to be chosen as one of the participants, but I was realistic enough to realize that probably wasn't my league. So I was genuinely surprised and elated to receive an invitation letter to the congress. Even my air fare was paid.

It was a thrill to attend the "1974 Lausanne Congress on World Evangelization." I was asked to be the secretary for the 18 of us from Bangladesh who met together for planning a future strategy for evangelistic outreach.

Never have I been in a gathering like that one. The devotional sessions sent the delegates soaring toward the heavenlies. Fuller Seminary professors (especially Ralph Winter and Donald McGavran) powerfully presented their case for the missiology of church growth. The participants went wild with applause when Francis Schaeffer stood up to deliver his penetrating lecture. Festo Kivengere's sermon on the Cross of Christ is forever seared into my memory. Added to the above, was the delight of having Cal Olson as my roommate in our small assigned hotel. Our times of prayer and eating delicious Swiss chocolates were spiritually and physically satisfying. It was a super time.

Back in Bangladesh things were not going so well for the Sheikh. He was busy consolidating power and, at the same time, demonstrating how inept he was in running the country. His popularity had fallen to an all time low. How could such a beloved leader self-destruct in a brief 3 1/2 years?

At 5 AM on the morning of August 15, 1975, we were awakened by what sounded like nearby blasts of tank cannons. Up to the roof, again. It was evident the action was taking place at the Sheikh's house about a mile distant from us. I called up a friend who could see the home of the prime minister from where he lived. He assured me that it was the Sheikh who was under attack. My friend and his family were all flat on the floor.

By 6:30 AM it was all over. Disgruntled soldiers had led the attack and succeeded in killing the Sheikh and every member of his family except for a daughter who was abroad. There was no outpouring of grief. Just stillness for days, as people tried to figure out what was going on.

From that early August morning in 1975 to the present, the Bangladesh political process has hobbled on. One additional head of state was assassinated, and another was incarcerated for several years. The daughter of one slain leader and the wife of the other, have held the top office in the land by turns for some time now, as first one party, then another, ascends to power through riot and election. Muslim Fundamentalists have begun to have a significant voice in politics. Somehow the enduring resilience of the average Bengali prevails. Through all the internal chaos, life goes on.

From 1975, the Muslim authorities in Bangladesh began to put pressure on missionaries. This was done by revoking or denying visas. In 1977, we had a major crisis. Dr. Viggo (Vic) Olsen, who authored *Daktar, Diplomat in Bangladesh,* is a special friend who not only assisted his own missionaries (Association of Baptist for World Evangelism), but also extended his efforts in behalf of every other mission society in the country.

Vic, at our request, graciously went to the American Ambassador and explained our visa problems. He was able to arrange for me to meet with the ambassador. How considerate and helpful this top U.S. official was to us. He immediately presented our case to the Bangladesh Department of Foreign Service as well as to the President. Apart from this, he set up a regular meeting of ambassadors which monitored the missionary visa issue. They diplomatically put pressure on the Bangladesh officials to ease up on us.

Humanly speaking, this type of assistance slowed down the efforts of the opposition group. It gave us extended time and freedom for ministry. It is only in recent years that the "missionary visa" is no longer granted or allowed. Only foreign non-government organizations (NGO's) are allowed in to do development work. They are closely monitored. A foreigner doing any type of overt Muslim evangelism is immediately expelled.

It must be said that U.S. official government pressure enabled us to carry on our outreach. How do I feel about this more refined type of "gunboat diplomacy" that I actively encouraged? Negative vibes. Who are we as missionaries to hide behind the skirts of the State Department? Is our trust more actively placed in the Lord, or the U.S. Government? What about the American concept of the separation of church and state? Should ambassadors go to bat for religious groups working overseas? And, finally, are we not trampling on the sensitivities of Muslims by such activities?

The other side of the coin. Foreign Muslim evangelizers are all over America. No restrictions are placed on their aggressive Islamic outreach. Why should we not have reciprocal privileges? America has assisted Bangladesh in countless ways. Is it asking too much for them to allow American missionaries to minister in their country in light of the massive help given to them? Then what about the U.N.-sponsored international Bill of Rights that promotes freedom of expression and religion?

These are the tough tensions of the real world in which we live. Hundreds, if not thousands of people have received eternal life because of the above stated actions. On the other hand, Muslims would respond by saying that these people have received eternal damnation! So, we press on, struggling with issues of ethics as applied to the thin line between temporal and eternal realities.

Fuller Seminary was like a mirage of water across the distant desert sands. Oh, so desirable, but just not real for me. No way could

I ever study at such an illustrious institution. But I did decide to do their five extension courses. It was a ton of work; listening to the tapes, reading the books and writing 25 page papers for each of the courses. Yet, it was exhilarating and extremely relevant to what I was doing. So I decided to take the plunge and seek to enroll in Fuller's residential Doctor of Missiology program. Amazingly, I was accepted, and we began to make plans for a two year study program.

By 1978, our team was beginning to see the first fruits of our "new" methodology. How exciting to see Muslims begin to place their faith in Christ. A personal concern I had related to my being bogged down in administration. Therefore, I requested the team to allow Julie and me to go to a totally unevangelized area upon return from our two years in the States. This proposal was accepted.

We had endured and enjoyed a full 4½ year third term. The highlight was the beginning of a process that would lead to small Muslim convert fellowships being planted throughout Bangladesh. The low point came during our vacation in Srinagar, Kashmir, when both Julie and Lyndi were bitten by a mad dog in the market. For the next 14 days they had to have an anti-rabies vaccine injected under the skin in their stomach region. That kind of put a damper on our holiday spirit. But as true troopers, they came through in great shape.

And, once again, it was time for home assignment.

Chapter 11

Fuller Seminary and Beyond

Our three months of deputation the summer of 1978 was a bit disheartening. My prophesy of support loss was fulfilled. Three churches just could not be comfortable with my studying at an institution like Fuller, even though I made my case that Fuller's School of World Mission was both evangelical and evangelistic. So we were faced with heavy tuition, as well as support requirements. I still do not fully understand how the Lord orchestrated it all, but every need was abundantly met.

Mrs. Mercedes Gribble is a selfless combination of Martha and Mary. She and her husband were able to purchase a rather large apartment complex in Pasadena for the use of students, particularly for missionaries who were studying at Fuller. We had a lovely two bedroom place, fully furnished even down to the cutlery and linen, for which we paid a minimum rent. What an oasis of peace for us during an extremely busy year. It was our first and only experience of living on a "missionary compound."

Fuller was a fascinating place to study. The academic demands were heavy, but I was still able to complete one and two-thirds years of work in one year. Julie was constantly at my side, assisting in research, typing, and hospitality. This, along with being Mom to 13-year-old Lyndi.

My entree at Fuller was helped by my article on Muslim evangelism which came out in a Fall 1978 issue of *Christianity Today*. Perhaps being 41 years old put me in a more senior category as well. The professors, without exception, were totally gracious and helpful. Chuck Kraft even invited me to be his teacher's assistant, an offer I had to refuse because of the academic load I was carrying. I insisted on adequate family times, plus closed books by 10 PM each night. Being a person who hates exams and loves to write, I was most fortunate that this was the assignment orientation at Fuller.

A landmark conference took place in Colorado Springs that Fall of 1978. Don McCurry gave leadership to a broadly representative group of people involved in Muslim outreach. The papers presented, along with the stimulating interaction, were exciting. I gave a case study on our Bangladesh ministry. Out of this gathering was birthed the Samuel Zwemer Institute. Don requested that I become the vice-chairman of the Board of Directors. Both Julie and I greatly enjoyed our involvement with Zwemer.

Another fun part of our time was to meet a young Bengali Muslim family at a Salvation Army outlet store. Miah and Rani and their young daughter were living in Pasadena. We had delicious rice and curry meals together. One weekend we did a sightseeing tour of San Francisco, staying overnight with their Muslim Bengali friends. Hopefully our Christian witness made some sort of impact in their lives.

Chuck Kraft, as my mentor, had agreed that I could write my dissertation in a format that would be ready to submit for publication. Most of my class papers fit in nicely as chapters of the dissertation. I really felt I was in great shape for the moment of high drama known in academia as a "doctoral defense." There before me were my three exalted professors. Imagine my sense of humiliation as one of them severely critiqued certain parts of my work. It was a real downer for me.

Actually, I had overreacted, because within a week the necessary corrections were made and an A received for my efforts. Amazingly, that book, *New Paths in Muslim Evangelism* (Baker Book House), was in print for sixteen years. In *New Paths*, I sought to set forth a paradigm shift in regard to a contextualized strategy for Muslim outreach. The book was somewhat controversial, but overall, it has been encouraging to see how the Lord has used it to stimulate new experimentation in evangelism.

Fuller required that I do a full nine month course of graduate theology which could be done at any accredited seminary. The nearest option with which I was comfortable was Azusa Pacific University. But as I moved toward the end of my year at Fuller, my mission requested that we move to Wheaton, Illinois, and become home director for one year. We agreed to do that if I could also be a full-time student at Wheaton Graduate School, which would enable me to complete my theology requirement for the Fuller doctorate. This time Wheaton had no trouble accepting me.

So eastward we headed in our rather inadequate Plymouth Volare station wagon. Soon we were settled into the comfortable suburban home owned by the mission. The mission office in Wheaton was reached by maneuvering down an alley not too far from the railway line. Wheaton College was on the other side of the tracks from us. I never did figure out who was on the right and who was on the wrong side of those tracks.

The kids at Wheaton sure did look and act young to this middle-ager. Everyone thought I was a professor. Theological studies, in contrast to missiological studies, have never turned me on. No new frontiers to break. But I survived, even though I was humbled by making a B+ in an undemanding Old Testament survey course in which the professor insisted on giving repetitive pop quizzes. A highlight of the time was initiating a long-term friendship with professors John Gration and Bill Wells. At the end of the nine months I was able to commence a process which converted Wheaton's "certificate" into an M.A. degree by taking one more course by extension and writing a thesis. This was later published as *Bridges to Islam* (Baker Book House). June 1980 saw us back at Fuller for graduation. The big surprise came during the ceremonies when I was called on stage to receive the "Donald McGavran Church Growth Award."

The Lausanne Congress on Evangelism Committee decided to sponsor a gathering of world leaders in Pattaya, Thailand, in the summer of 1980. I was invited to be a delegate and to make a seminar presentation. This conference dove-tailed nicely with our return journey to Bangladesh. My expenses at the congress were paid, as were Julie's because of her rather minimal responsibility of being a secretary for the Islam track. Lyndi just enjoyed having a 5-star vacation for ten days.

Why 5-star? Well, the huge, even palatial, hotel where we met was something else. Not only was it grandiose and right on the ocean, but each meal was buffet-style with huge spreads of food laid out on long tables which were beautifully decorated with vases of Thai orchids. Several delegates mentioned they had pangs of guilt as they discussed subjects relating to poverty and the sad plight of the refugees, particularly those a few hundred miles north of us on the Thai-Cambodia border. The organizers got a special deal on the hotel. But some of us felt it would have been prudent to have even paid more and have met in a place with a much lower profile.

Our next flight took us from Bangkok to Manila, Philippines. There we underwent the excruciating process of leaving our 15 year-old daughter in the dorm at Faith Academy. This was our first separation as a family. The next morning we called Lyndi prior to our departure for Bangladesh and she tearfully mumbled (in Bengali so the other girls would not understand), "Dad, I don't want to stay here. I want to go with you and Mom back to Bangladesh." Near to a breaking point, I asked her to give it her best shot. She graciously agreed to stay on. We had explained to her that her part in our ministry at this time was to "make it" at boarding school so we could continue our work in Bangladesh. If she couldn't, she came first and we would return to the States as a family. We left Manila with a heavy spirit.

A New Frontier

What a crummy night was in store for me right after our arrival back in Dhaka. I tossed and turned throughout the long, black hours that seemed interminable. Half of my family support team was gone. We faced an unknown future in the totally unevangelized town of Ampara (a pseudonym), far to the West. It was hot and humid. Seemingly, God was on vacation and not returning my calls. Misery, plain unadulterated misery.

But amazingly, the next morning the sun did shine and God did reappear on house calls. Julie was still at my right hand. Yes, life would be bearable. So plans were made and we began the long day's trek westward in a dilapidated truck laden down with our furniture.

Ampara is a small, sleepy district town which serves as an administrative center for over one million people. To the best of our knowledge, there had been no Muslim converts in the area for at least fifty years. Ampara is a center for the *Baul* Sufi sect, a group whose doctrine is somewhat of a syncretism between Islam and Hinduism.

Our goal in Ampara was to use a team of four couples to implement our culturally sensitive approach to Muslim evangelism. We all lived in rather unpretentious places rented from Muslims. Julie and I were in a three-room house (each room being 12 foot by 12 foot), plus small spaces for the kitchen and bathroom facilities. Shades of Manikganj followed us in regard to our "commode" being a hole, flanked on either side by a brick. When doused with adequate water, it emptied out into a septic tank. A 55 gallon drum provided water for a pour bath.

The house was super hot six months of the year. Cycle rickshaws provided our transportation. The hardest moments came from unruly kids who delighted to be innovative in finding ways to disturb the peace of the foreigners.

Stored deeply in my emotional bank is the day I reached bottom in Ampara. It had been a month since we left our tearful daughter in Manila. Because of the poor postal system, we had heard nothing from her. I was being torn up inside. One afternoon I went into our bathroom, closed the door, and wept my heart out. I had experienced an emotional amputation. The Lord and time would be the healing agents that would allow me to press on. Of course, the soon arrival of a happy letter from Lyndi helped immensely.

In the early 70's a young Bengali had walked into my office in Dhaka and startled me by saying, "Thank you for bringing me from darkness to light." I knew that Yakub was a Muslim convert and had been recently baptized in the local church, but I had no active part in his conversion, at least as far as I knew. Yakub then told me of his curiosity being activated by the sight of a tall foreigner selling books in a downtown area of Dhaka. He purchased some literature, read it, went to the Southern Baptist reading room whose address was on one of the tracts, met a national Christian, and was led to Christ. Quite a story. I had the privilege of being that first link in the chain of events which eventuated in Yakub's conversion.

Yakub has been ministering for Christ ever since. He married an outstanding Christian girl, and became one of Bangladesh's most effective evangelists among Muslims. What a privilege it was to have Yakub working with us as the national component to our Ampara group. We were all one team, but one of the couples and Yakub were part of a sister mission which was seconded to the new outreach.

Our strategy centered around "reading centers" in areas accessible by a bus or train ride. We felt it wise to be out of Ampara town and into the larger villages. Our centers were open mainly on the weekly market days when large crowds of Bengalis came into the villages to buy and sell goods. The rooms we rented were basic, often without electricity. They were attractively decorated with an Islamic motif. We sat on mats on the floor and interacted with Muslims about the higher issues of God and His plan for sinful man. We used an effective correspondence course to stimulate ongoing personal contact with the Muslims.

Yakub and I ministered in two of the outreaches which were accessed by a 45 minute train ride. We would go out at 9 AM and return by 10 PM, assuming the evening train would cooperate, schedule wise. Those were long, hot, often discouraging days, particularly the first year. Yakub was, and is, a brilliant communicator of the Gospel. I would often marvel at the wisdom the Lord has given this relatively uneducated (in a formal sense) man. Slowly, in these and the other centers, we began to see fruit. Yakub was the key to all that was accomplished.

Soon we needed a training center to disciple the new believers. We rented a small three-room house in a convenient location in Ampara Town. Many have been the overnight sessions that God has used in that training center to bring Muslims to a point of vital surrender to Christ. By the early 80's, the Lord was doing a new thing throughout Bangladesh, a work that has continued to the present.

Dr. Ali

How do I introduce Dr. Ali into my memoirs? In many people's lives there come unexpected and unique relational encounters. Dr. Ali was mine. In 1980, following our arrival in Ampara, we kept hearing of this devout Muslim college professor. All of the students kept referring to him as such a nice person. One morning I went over to the local college to meet him. Into the waiting room bounced this bubbly, effervescent, middle-aged professor of English. Ali greeted me as a long-lost brother. It was evident we were headed for an unusual relationship. After a brief conversation, Julie and I were cordially invited for tea at the Ali home. Little did I know that I had just come into contact with the most gracious, ethical, and dedicated Muslim that I have ever met.

Ali was a home-grown Ampara product. Following graduation from a local college, he attended the most prestigious university in Bangladesh from where he received his Ph.D. degree. He returned to Ampara to teach and to establish a small folklore institute. This institution provided Ali with an academic outlet for his many research projects. Particularly this was true as it related to Ali being perhaps the chief researcher of the *Baul* sect. Each year the television crews would journey west to Ampara to record the happenings at the annual *Baul* festival. Ali was the organizer of this well-publicized event. In his spare time he wrote many books and articles, almost all relating to the rural Sufi-type (mystical) Muslim.

And so I had discovered my first intimate Muslim friend, one I have written extensively about in my books. Quickly our relationship progressed in the social, academic, and religious areas of life. We spent many hours together drinking milky tea and eating delicious Bengali sweets. Academically, he led me into the world of Mystical Islam, a world I hardly knew existed before I met Ali. Religiously, we spent hundreds of hours quietly seeking to resolve the doctrinal differences that stubbornly separate us as devout followers of God's Word, which for me is the Bible and for Ali is the Quran.

Though Ali is so esteemed among his fellow Muslims, few know him as I do. Apart from his family, Ali's friends all used the honorific, somewhat distant form of Bengali in addressing him. One day he said to me, "Phil, why not use the intimate pronoun in talking to each other? You are my brother. I am closer to you than any other person." A real honor!

In Muslim homes in Bangladesh, the sitting room is for meeting guests. The bedrooms are where family and the closest of friends sit. Julie and I were always ushered back into the inner part of the home. There we saw real love in action among family members.

Ali's intelligent wife is a professor at the local girl's college. One sharp and handsome son has a Master's Degree and is profitably employed. Another son had been incorrectly medicated when he was 18 months old and, therefore, is somewhat retarded, yet very sensitive and loving. Ali's daughter, graced with classical beauty and a provocative nature, was always on center stage. Years later, she was granted a Ford Foundation Scholarship which enabled her to obtain a Masters Degree at Harvard University's prestigious John F. Kennedy School of Public Administration. Ali's mother and father added stability and direction to the swirl of activities and chatter that were omnipresent in the home.

Ali provided me with impeccable credentials for entry into the upper-crust of Muslim society in Ampara. We attended functions together as well as visited the homes of the highest government officials. Once he arranged for me to speak (in Bengali) to a district-wide gathering of all the top police officials. With a twinkle in my eye, I encouraged them to be upright guardians of the community, personally shunning all bribery and corruption. They were delighted to hear an American speak in their language. After that, I only received the highest respect from this strata of people who could have been our team's arch antagonists. I was a friend of Dr. Ali. Nothing else need be said, or investigated.

In a land where this might be expected, never once did Ali directly or indirectly seek to obtain a loan or "gift" from me. Our reciprocal giving over the years has been about even, though I did orchestrate his being invited as a "Visiting Scholar" at the Harvard Center for World Religion. Harvard University paid his air fare and all expenses for a three month stint which most Bengalis could only fantasize about. It was a privilege to do this for my special friend.

Now, to exegete the tough part of our relationship. Ali is a "godly" person. I remember once watching him as a storm was starting to move across the fields toward us. He threw his hands heavenward and repeatedly cried out into the wind, "*Al hamdulillah,*" i.e.,: "Praise the Lord, Praise the Lord." Ali is a man in sync with the God of creation. His devotional life is impeccable. The five-times-a-day prayer ritual, to Ali, is not a burden, but rather a joy. Never have I seen him miss a prayer time. Many have been the occasions we have prayed together, though he was always aware that I prayed as a Christian.

Ali's personal purity is absolute. He has told me of being sexually propositioned in various countries during his travels to academic meetings. His response was to assure the ladies that he could never deny Allah or his family in such a degrading manner. In all of our times together, I have never seen a hint of a personal compromise in his integrity. He also has an amazing way of being constantly interested in others with a depth of sincerity seldom found among those of my own religious tradition. Though he would have reason for being proud of his significant accomplishments in life, I have only noted a humble spirit in his demeanor.

So what do you do with a "God seeker" who comes out looking better than most evangelical Christians, at least better than many I know? Ali has appreciated my Christian testimony. So much so that he says, "Phil, the result of knowing you has led me to be a better Muslim." Wow! Reverse evangelism.

And so, one more enigma for me to ponder on life's pathway. Both Ali and I are desirous for each other to convert. Our prayers are to that end. One thing I do know. My life has been made much richer because of walking into the lives of Dr. Ali and his lovely family. Muslims extraordinaire!

A New Direction

During 1981, Julie and I, along with Dick Walton of SEND International, conducted a survey trip through Mindanao, the island in the Philippines where some five million Muslims reside. Our mission was keen to open a new field. OMF and SEND suggested a three mission consortium by which we could pool resources and thereby make a greater impact on the Magindanaon people group. Among these one million Muslims there were only ten known converts and not one of these continued to live as salt and light among his or her own people.

At the time of the survey we had no thought of leading our mission's team into Muslim ministry in the Philippines. But little by little the Bangladesh government was starting to crack down on all who were engaged in evangelism. Because of this, our team had decided I could no longer write on subjects relating to Islam. Also, the visa situation was precarious. It would be difficult, if not impossible, to travel to seminars and speaking engagements outside Bangladesh. Added to the above was the fact that we had an excellent team in place who could cover for my absence without any problem. They would be able to exercise their own gifts of leadership much more effectively without my rather forceful personality hovering over them.

Ampara? Could I spend the rest of my life dressed in baggy national dress, sporting a distasteful salt and pepper beard, and enduring the ever-present taunts of the cheeky youth? Was I getting soft after 20 years in Bangladesh? Did my Fuller doctorate reprogram me in some sub-conscious manner? At 45 years of age, was I undergoing a mid-life crisis?

In light of all this, I wrote an extensive letter of pros and cons about changing fields to the Philippines. This was sent to 25 friends and supporting churches who were asked to pray over the options and get back to me. Their counsel and prayer guidance were needed at this crucial juncture of our lives. All but one response suggested a green light for the big move. The one hesitant church assured us of their full support if we did go to the Philippines. Julie's position was rather neutral, assuring me of her total backing and her commitment to follow me in whatever direction I felt the Lord leading. So, the decision was reached, not without a great deal of prayer and soul-searching. To the Philippines we would go.

The Cancer Scare

In the Fall of 1982, while we were still mulling over the decision, Julie had a hysterectomy at the Memorial Christian

Hospital, an excellent missionary facility operated by the Association of Baptists for World Evangelism, located at the southern tip of Bangladesh. It seemed to be a straightforward surgical procedure done by a competent American surgeon. As soon as Julie recovered, we returned to Ampara.

A few days later, we received a letter from the surgeon which turned our lives upside down. An excerpt follows:

> *The pathology report says that Julie has a frank malignancy. About that there is no question and no equivocation. My first recommendation is that you immediately make arrangements to head for home. Please do not use just any old hospital once home. Go to one of the very best.... Do not delay in making your arrangements to get home NOW.*

We sat on the bed and read and reread the long letter of explanation and exhortation. Somehow life's tapestry now assumed a look of complication and confusion. To our finite eyes, the design had gone askew.

What now? The pathologist suggested that the cancer may well have spread throughout the body, perhaps originating in the breast. Time was of the utmost essence. We had to get moving in a most dramatic way. Our emotions were in a swirl. Hand in hand, we bowed in prayer. We asked for God's enabling grace to so permeate us that, even as Julie faced possible death, we could have an overcoming testimony to our fellow missionaries, new convert believers, and to the Ali family. It was time to portray in living color the message we had so often preached. Our actions and words in the crucible would be worth more than a thousand sermons and dozens of authored books.

In order to preserve the emotional force of those last few days in Ampara, let me quote a paragraph I wrote shortly after we returned to the States.

> *Life went into a spin as we packed our belongings in drums, made travel arrangements, turned over Mission leadership responsibilities, and had prayer with the leaders of the emerging church. A very touching and meaningful*

> experience was how Professor Ali and his Muslim family
> interacted with us. Ali stayed with me almost the whole time.
> His family visited frequently bringing sweets. Each evening
> Ali went through the Muslim prayer ritual and then bowed
> and prayed, with tears coursing down his cheeks, for Julie's
> healing. Ali accompanied us to the airport where at 9
> o'clock in the morning eleven of us sat down and ate the five
> chickens, Bangladeshi bread and special sweets he had
> brought. It is a great joy and privilege to be Dr. Ali's
> intimate friend. On the last night together, we shared our
> faith with each other for over three hours. It hurt me deeply
> to realize this sincere God-seeker who is so gracious has
> missed the only path by which he can find spiritual reality
> and eternal life.

Along with the Alis, our missionaries, both in Ampara and
Dhaka went all out to ease our burdens and to be helpful in every
way. The really tough part was to stop by Manila and pull Lyndi out
of her twelfth grade. We sat with all her dorm friends the one
evening we were there and listened as the girls tearfully told of all
that Lyndi meant to them. Then on the plane flying out of Manila the
tears flowed as we read the precious notes of love that only high-
school girls can write. Lyndi's life was in disarray. We felt terribly
for her.

Our fantastic church, Highland Park Baptist in Detroit, had made
complete arrangements for us. A lovely condo (with swimming pool
privileges) was loaned to us by Alice Marderosian. Two cars were
supplied. Free schooling at our church's high school was provided
for Lyndi. Appointments with doctors were arranged. What a church!

In just a week after our arrival, word came back that lab work on
the specimen we had brought to the States in a baby food jar (which
caused no little consternation to the customs inspector in Hawaii at 2
AM) was proved conclusively NOT malignant. It appeared that the
Bengali lab technician in Dhaka had attached the slides of someone
else's breast cancer to our specimen. Julie's "all okay" uterine report
must have gone to the lady with the breast cancer. A comedy of
errors with dire consequences for the other lady.

And so, three relieved but traumatized persons sat on the floor of the condo bedroom and tried to work through all the happenings of the previous two weeks. We felt a keen sense of embarrassment for the trouble we had caused the saints, though all assured us of their delight upon hearing of Julie's "healing." Lyndi took it the hardest as she had no desire to enter a new school where she knew no one. We had no choice but to remain in Detroit for a year of furlough.

Pilgrimage, at times, can be a painful process. But the end is eminently worthwhile. We had no option but to continue on the journey. That was both by compulsion and by choice.

Chapter 12

Harvard and the Philippines

Each afternoon that I was home during Lyndi's senior year, a certain ritual would take place. Our tearful daughter would come through the door and throw herself on the couch. Bringing her a glass of Coke, I would sit for 30 minutes and listen intently to her recitation of hurts brought about by real and/or imagined problems with her classmates. Lyndi had gone from popularity within her MK subculture to being a non-entity in a wealthy suburban American school. How does a kid break into well-established relational cliques in October of one's senior year? The administration and faculty were excellent in their sensitivity, but Lyndi's peers left somewhat to be desired.

Yet, through all the pain, Lyndi was able to persevere and enjoy a happy graduation in June of 1983. A few months later she and I flew out to Los Angeles. As I installed Lyndi in her Biola University dorm room, I gave her three final exhortations: (1) follow Biola's rules; (2) remember you are the Lord's; and (3) keep in mind you are a Parshall. A joyful and fulfilling four years at Biola followed, culminating in her graduation in 1987 with a major in sociology.

Our year of furlough was intense. Apart from numerous church meetings, highlights were: teaching a course at Wheaton Graduate School; speaking in chapels at Gordon-Conwell and Westminster seminaries; giving a series of messages to the annual gathering of SEND International missionaries and supporters in Michigan; plus being one of two keynote speakers at the annual meeting of the

American Society of Missiology. *Bridges To Islam* (Baker) was released in 1983, while *Beyond the Mosque* (Baker) was nearing completion.

One day while reading *Christianity Today,* I noticed an advertisement which solicited applications from pastors who would be desirous of taking a semester refresher at Harvard Divinity School. This "Merrill Fellowship" program is financed by a son of one of the founders of Merrill-Lynch, the famous investment corporation. Considering my "investment" would be limited to the cost of a postage stamp, I decided to go for it. Surely there was a bit of presumptuousness on my part. Who was I, an evangelical missionary, to be applying to the most academically recognized and liberal seminary in America?

But, it did sound like an interesting opportunity. Later, I found out that the semester I applied, they only accepted four out of 36 applicants. Never had a missionary been a part of the program. I still vividly recall receiving the phone call from Harvard informing me of my acceptance for the Fall semester of 1983. What a thrill!

Ten different friends in the Boston area sought to find us a furnished apartment for the short period between September and December. After much searching, they found a small attic apartment with an outside stairway going up the three stories. The warm fellowship we enjoyed with the Christian owners more than compensated for our basic accommodation. All of this provided a touch of humility for us as we walked among the high and mighty.

Julie and I were somewhat overawed as we first entered the imposing campus of Harvard University. The massive central library houses over seven million books. Another three million are to be found in satellite libraries within the various graduate schools. In the center of the campus is the high profile New England style "Memorial Church." Its frequently held services and hourly bell-ringing could give one the impression that God is given some significant notoriety at Harvard. Tradition best explains a form that in the 1600s had a great deal of meaning. Unfortunately today, God is more a peripheral ornament than a centerpiece of reality at Harvard, although it is amusing to gaze upon the words "What is man that Thou are mindful of Him?" emblazoned deep in the facade of the huge philosophy building.

Over to the far side of the campus one finds several buildings which house the Harvard Divinity School. I was pleasantly surprised that first day when we four "Fellows" were greeted warmly by the dean and his assistant. They assured us we could take any courses we wanted throughout the entire university system. This could be done for credit or audit. There would be no charge and they would take care of all the registration procedures. Beyond that, we each could expect a check for $2,200, for living expenses.

We would also be considered "Harvard Alumni" at the end of the semester. This was confirmed later by my receiving repeated requests from the alumni office for financial donations. More interestingly, it meant I have become a member of the "Harvard Club" here in the Philippines which is an association of the multi-millionaire Filipino graduates of Harvard. I have yet to come up with the required money to attend one of their dinners at the ostentatious and elite Polo Club.

And finally, the frosting on the cake. We were given free access to the Harvard Faculty Club. It is all the name implies, an ivy-covered building that houses a huge book-lined room of overstuffed chairs and two large coffee urns. Slouch onto a couch with a cup of coffee, *Wall Street Journal* in hand, a pipe dangling from your lips, and you become an instant member of the lofty world of academia.

More germane to the pragmatic world of the Parshalls was the provision of lunches in the Club's lovely dining room, or the choice of a sandwich and soup bar in the basement. The prices were quite reasonable from 11 AM to 3 PM and totally astronomical from 6 PM on. Many were our friends we thrilled with a lunch in the Harvard Faculty Club. Special were meals with Wilfred Cantwell Smith and Bishop Kenneth Cragg, together with their spouses. These men are two of the world's greatest Islamicists. For $100 per year our club privileges could live on. But, alas, such is but a dream some 10,000 miles distant in our country of choice.

Out of a desire to see if I could hack it academically at Harvard, I took *Worldview* and *Islam* as credit courses and then audited

Pilgrimages and *History of Religion*. My A- and B+ would have been full A's at Fuller (my ego says), but no matter, it was a fun experience.

The other "Fellows" included one male and two female Fellows. Kevin was the pastor of a large Seventh Day Adventist Church. We had a real affinity together as he had a high regard for Fuller Seminary. Kevin's faith in his Church was deeply shaken through the allegation of Ellen White's plagiarism. He felt his sense of integrity suggested that he may have to leave the pastorate. I took no satisfaction in seeing Kevin hurt so sincerely and so deeply.

Jane was the moderator for a group of Boston liberal churches. She met her husband looking out from her apartment window into the window of a nearby apartment. Somehow they breached the gap. Jane gave us a copy of her husband's newly published book. I am sure it was brilliant writing as I could not understand what it was all about. But I was able to compliment her on finding a husband capable of such profound thoughts.

The fourth "Fellow," Sue, was the most interesting of all. She was a non-Theist Unitarian pastor who had applied at least three times for the Fellowship. Immediately, she squared off against me by approvingly citing her friend's good judgment that she would rather have her son watch pornography than tune in to a television evangelist. I knew I had my work cut out for me. One of my goals at Harvard was to make Sue see evangelicals (not particularly TV evangelists!) in a new and better light.

Each Wednesday the four of us had a private lunch with a senior seminary professor. What fun to rap informally with the likes of George Rupp, now the president of Columbia University, and Harvey Cox, the religion "expert" that *Time* magazine and everyone else loves to quote. How down to earth were these professors. We called them by their first names. They had "arrived." No need for pretension.

To my surprise, the four of us Fellows quickly forged a deep bond of friendship. Others in the Divinity School commented on this as rather unique. Yes, I did make significant progress with Sue. She relaxed with Julie and me to the point that we received a gracious note from her at the end of the semester. Now if only I can get her to believe there is a God!

Julie was allowed to sit in on my classes, which made it all the more special. We never, in any way, felt discriminated against because of being evangelicals. Much to my surprise, I was asked to be the speaker at the Divinity School's Thanksgiving Chapel service which turned out to have the largest attendance of the semester. I gave a copy of *Bridges to Islam* to Dean George Rupp who read it on a plane going to a meeting. He mentioned it to me later with appreciative comments.

We were also invited to functions at the Harvard Center for World Religion. It was through these contacts that I was able to get Dr. Ali accepted as a visiting scholar in the Center. Our time ended with a gourmet lunch with Mr. Merrill in a private dining room at the Faculty Club. He is a gracious, but highly opinionated person. I distinctly remember his lament at how little impact Harvard Divinity School and other liberal seminaries are making on the masses!

Harvard has a policy to hire the most qualified and intellectual person in the world to fill each of their faculty positions. What a goal of excellence! I found the professors to be awesome in brainpower. At times, they left me breathless in their presentations. And yet, I often thought of the words of Jesus as He put worldly wisdom in perspective by saying we must become as little children if we desire to enter the Kingdom of God. As a short-term "insider" I saw nothing that would make me desire to be a Christian of liberal persuasion. I said a fond adieu to Harvard, with my evangelicalism solidly intact.

Manila

And now, our thoughts turned towards the Philippines. Adequate funds were not coming in for our needs in regard to getting settled into Manila. This was particularly true as it related to the $10,000 required for a second-hand car. At the last moment, a small foundation that donates "seed money" for new ministries sent us a check for $15,000. What a burden was lifted from us.

January 10, 1984, we arrived at the Manila International Airport. Our new pilgrimage had begun. Friends who met us at the airport told us of the availability of one duplex apartment in the area we had chosen. The housing market was extremely tight. Dropping off our suitcases at a missionary guesthouse, we went and looked at the apartment. It had inadequacies that made us have a measure of doubt about its suitability. But, with alterations, we were able to make it into a comfortable home-cum-office. We have lived in this duplex far longer than in any other residence during our married life. Our landlord is uniquely fair in his rent demands.

We live in a high crime area bounded by two large squatter settlements. Numerous break-ins and three killings have occurred within 50 yards of our place. Friends have suggested we have guardian angels watching over us as we have only had one purse snatching during these years. Betty, our street-smart house helper, carefully screens all who come to the gate. She has been a great asset to our ministry. We have been able to walk away for up to six months and be assured that our apartment will be kept in excellent condition. Heavy rains frequently inundate our driveway. Flood waters have entered the house on a number of occasions, but Betty has it all cleaned within hours of the water's receding. It has been our privilege to ease Betty's financial burdens over the years. She has raised seven kids, most of the time without any assistance from her irresponsible husband.

As far as I can research, it appears that I am the first full-time minister, (missionary or national), to ever engage in evangelism among the 50,000 Muslims of Manila. They have been a totally neglected peoples group over the centuries. When we decided to come to the Philippines, I made a commitment to the Lord that I would not become an armchair strategist, but rather would be involved directly with Muslims. This is not because of any masochistic tendency on my part.

As a matter of record, I must state that I find face to face Muslim evangelism to be a hard route to take. Having one's message constantly demeaned and rejected is not easy on one's sense of ministerial fulfillment. What drives me is simply the biblical-based conviction that Muslims are lost, along with the statistical reality that few of the one billion adherents to Islam have had an adequate opportunity to hear a clear presentation of the Gospel.

During my first year in Manila, I would take a bus down to the Muslim area and sit on the steps of the different mosques, seeking to develop friendships. It was a miserable twelve months. The Muslims did not want me there any more than we as Christians would appreciate their evangelists camping out on our church steps at 12 noon on Sundays. Over the years, I have come to see the mosque and its immediate vicinity as an area of dynamic spirituality to the Muslim. I should respect their space and only do that which I am invited to do by those who are present. This usually includes listening while they try to convert me! Even so, much can be gained by taking the humble position of a learner.

Following that uncomfortable year, the Lord opened up a 12 foot by 15 foot storefront room ideally located between two Islamic communities. There is a constant flow of Muslims walking within a foot of our double doors and attractive picture window. The room has been decorated with appropriate cultural and religious symbols. Twenty stools are arranged so Muslims can be seated as they watch the two-hour *Jesus* video which is shown Tuesday through Friday afternoons. Hundreds from the nearby community have seen this film. They are particularly gripped by the powerful crucifixion scene.

There are thirteen Muslim dialects among the five million Muslim Filipinos. Each people group has a distinct dialect. Therefore, I stock literature in multiple languages. I place two tables of books and tracts on the sidewalk just outside the Center. Chairs are provided for those who would like to sit and chat.

Once I reminisced about the Center and its immediate environs:

> *The street was dark and isolated. I had just moved the Christian literature from the tables into the cupboards. It was 7:30, and time to close down the Reading Center, which is located in the midst of the Muslim community in inner-city Manila. As I put boards over the display window and closed the double doors, I glanced down at the repaired bolt which brought memories of the phone call telling me of the attempted break in. Were the thieves willing to risk a jail sentence to steal only a fan, or were they trying to send a message to the Christian missionary who had blatantly invaded their turf?*

Divine Threads Within A Human Tapestry

As I walked down the deserted sidewalk, I came to a small bridge over an unbelievably filthy canal. I looked to the right and surveyed the Islamic Center in the distance. Over 20,000 Muslims are packed into an area measuring about half a square mile. Delinquent Muslims move about in broad daylight robbing, raping, and killing. Then they quickly return, secure in the belief that the police and military will not follow them into their "city of refuge." Much to the surprise of two cop-killers, 200 policemen recently violated this precedent and went door to door in the community with the result that they were able to arrest the wounded suspects.

Closer to where I was standing on the bridge I observed scores of thin plywood shanties precariously hanging out over the murky waters of the canal. In each of these six-foot-square hovels are living as many as eight Muslim family members.

Towering over this maze of restless humanity is the minaret of the famous Golden Mosque. It was from the top of this same tower that a deranged Muslim in a midnight foray of madness began wildly shooting everyone in sight. After he had thrown a few grenades, he was successfully subdued and arrested.

As I walked over the bridge into the crowded Quiapo square, I was accosted by the "Christian" contributions to the religiously mixed area. First, I saw the short-term hotel which caters to the Eros drives of youth. For two dollars, a couple can enjoy the facilities of a bed and a bathroom for three hours.

Then there were the ever-present peddlers of pornography. In the midst of the stench and deprivation of poverty, one can take a flight into the fantasy of sexual experience. For a measly ten cents, explicit comic books offer escape... but only an escape from Purgatory to Hell. Moral standards become anesthetized and it's only a short step away to thievery and drug abuse.

Finally, I made my way to the bus stand, and as I did, I paused in front of the Quiapo Catholic Church. Outside were the scores of vendors offering holy water, candles, statues of Mary, and of course, lottery tickets baptized in luck because they were sold on the church verandah. Inside, hundreds of the devout jostled against each other as they moved toward the glass-encased, six-foot statue of the Black Nazarene. Each believer went directly to the feet of Jesus which protruded from the coffin. There they touched, kissed, and rubbed the painted toes of the dead Savior. In their wrinkled faces could be seen eyes of hope filled with looks of dire despair.

Just outside the church I boarded the bus and sat pensively viewing the crowd. Three cute 13-year-old girls were animatedly discussing the day's events. Held on their arms were garlands of flowers which they were selling to Catholics who would then take them home and place them lovingly over the head of their patron saint. One of the girls became excited and angry as she told of one of the happenings of the day. As her voice rose, she roughly caressed her breasts several times. Now, there is anger and shame. Tomorrow she may be unable to resist the lure of the pesos for selling her precious body.

The bus lurched forward.

Goodnight, Quiapo.

Goodnight, Christians.

Goodnight, Muslims.

I'll see you tomorrow... in the night.

Has it been worth all the hassles of the past years to "hang in" with the witness of the Reading Center? The afternoon sun bears down, harshly penetrating even the bedspread I hang up to shade the chairs and tables of literature. Pollution from the never-ending flow of smoke-belching busses and taxis has given me an intermittent cough. The harsh cacophony of traffic makes it difficult, and sometimes impossible, to carry on a conversation.

All for what? Hundreds of pieces of literature have been sold. The *Jesus* film has been shown scores of times. Many intense conversations about Christ have taken place. But, so far, there has only been one convert from this outreach.

Mila was a young, discouraged Muslim girl contemplating suicide. She had found life depressing and hostile. One afternoon she was walking by our Center and was amazed to see two foreign men sitting behind tables of literature. Mila looked into the doorway and noticed a foreign woman who immediately struck up a conversation with her.

This sequence was the beginning of a deep relationship between Mila and the missionary lady. Within a relatively short few weeks, Mila was led to the Lord. Over these past years, she has grown tremendously in the faith. Her greatest triumph was to bring her sister to salvation in Christ. Mila's vibrant witness of zeal and courage have inspired many. Filipino Muslims have boasted to me that none of the one million people of Mila's tribe have ever become a Christian. By God's power, Mila is one that has. A special trophy of grace.

Manila is a megalopolis of ten million people. It is a harsh city of heat, floods, pollution, gridlocked traffic, robberies, violence, drugs, alcohol abuse, abandoned families, homosexual, heterosexual, and pedophilic promiscuity. Experts have suggested that one-third of Manila's residents live below the poverty level, mostly being housed in terrible slums that are omnipresent throughout the city. Such deprivation leads directly to thousands of young people being engaged in some form of crime. Visitors are amazed to find even the smallest shops have armed guards to protect them from thieves. Where but Manila can one visit a McDonald's where the doors are opened by security men armed with automatic rifles!

Filipinos have, in the last few decades, experienced a sexual revolution, at least partly fueled by Western magazines and films. Sociologists ponder the dominance of the female in home and society as a cause of widespread homosexuality. Gays openly flout their sexual preferences in parades and beauty contests. Our Filipino house helper has twin sons, one of whom is a blatant homosexual with long, flowing hair, and totally effeminate gestures. The other twin is thoroughly masculine. Same home influences. And so the arguments rage on concerning the influence of nature and nurture.

Massage parlors provide a legitimate front for illegitimate back room prostitution. "Short-term" motels with drive-in private garages provide a discreet environment for after-office-hour affairs. Discos with pretty young "hospitality girls" are found in every neighborhood.

During the period when Subic Naval Base was a dominant force in U.S. defense policy, as well as in the Philippine political scene, Julie, Lyndi, and I spent a night in Olongapo, the city just outside the base. The aircraft carrier Kittyhawk was in port along with its accompanying ships. Some 15,000 lustful American sailors were prowling the streets while 15,000 attractive Filipinos sought to pull them into their bars or massage parlors. Sodom and Gomorra come to life in jarring reality. Around 15 of the sailors opted for the wholesome atmosphere of the Christian Servicemen's Center where we spent the night. How delighted we were a few years later when the Philippine Senate courageously voted to close down the remaining outposts of American military influence in the Philippines. At minimum, this act put a few prostitutes out of business.

There will come a day of terrible heart searching when the full extent of the AIDS reality is discovered. Inadequate testing procedures ensure that the spread of the virus continues unencumbered. The use of condoms is actively discouraged by the Roman Catholic Church leaders who see it religiously as an unacceptable form of birth control, rather than as a deterrent to AIDS and venereal disease.

How can these blatant forces of immorality rage like wildfire in a country where conservative values once reigned? Is it even conceivable that the only "Christian" nation in Asia vies with Thailand as the sex capital of the region? Where is the Church? Has it no voice, no influence?

That is a hard question to answer. Basically, it seems Filipinos are happy to engage in the ritual of the church without incorporating its reality into their lives. Definitely, Filipinos are overwhelmingly religious. Churches are packed. The Charismatic movement (both Catholic and Protestant) generates tremendous enthusiasm among the masses. To be "born again" is a badge of a higher plane of spirituality to most. But the piercing question is, "Why so little impact on the everyday morality of the people?" The Cardinal makes his pious pontifications to the 85 percent of the population which are Catholic. But it almost seems like the Church has lost its anticipation of change. A peaceful co-existence with sin has muted its prophetic voice. Perhaps the Church leadership is just old and tired. Complacency and compromise have replaced vigor and vision.

In reality, are the sins and failures of the Filipinos greater than those of Americans? Could not I list a similar catalog of inadequacies for the residents of Los Angeles or San Francisco? There are definite similarities. One glaring distinction relates to economics. Poverty in the Philippines drives many to unethical conduct, such as bribery, thievery, and prostitution. For a segment of Filipinos, need motivates toward sin; whereas in America, greed often is the precipitating factor. In the West, the mode is a bit cleaner, i.e., through stolen bank cards and computer intrusion. A realist, therefore, concludes that depravity knows no ethnic boundaries.

As with an evaluation of any people, there is always an alternative response to evil. So many Filipinos are beautiful people. Physically, they keep themselves clean and neat. They take pride in "smooth inter-personal relationships." Fun-loving, personable, smiling, they are an accepting, gracious race. Some of the chief movers of society are women. They are to be found in high level positions throughout the business world. From President, to owners of small grocery stores, and everything in between, the woman is a committed, stable worker.

Filipino women, by the hundreds of thousands, toil arduously outside their country in an effort to make life more bearable for their extended family left behind in the Philippines. These long periods of separation have taken a serious toll on family life. Divorce is not legally permitted, so the fleshly response of many is to have an affair on the side.

While women work as maids and entertainers, unskilled Filipino men are hired as drivers and construction workers. There are exceptions, but these are the most available job opportunities in the Middle East. At the present time, 18,000 Filipinos are in prisons abroad. Many have found it impossible to conform to the puritanical standards of morality so rigidly enforced in Islamic contexts. Regrettably, a large number of young, attractive girls serving in Muslim homes have suffered sexual abuse. A controversial incident has highlighted the plight of a 16-year-old Filipino maid in the United Arab Emirates who stabbed her 85-year-old employer 37 times as he tried to rape her. She was sentenced to death by a UAE Islamic court, but, under pressure from Western human rights groups, this Muslim girl had her sentence reduced to 100 lashes and one year in prison.

One of the great joys of these years has been the privilege of working with Filipinos in the ministry. The Diliman Bible Church, where we attend, has caught the vision of Muslim outreach. They have four varied ministries in Islamic areas of Manila. Also, a tentmaker from our church is making a significant impact as a social worker in Mindanao. She has spearheaded a foundation which seeks to demonstrate practical expressions of love through community development projects.

Presently, most of the Muslim areas of Manila have some type of Christian witness in them, almost all of which are sanctioned by local residents. My more overtly evangelistic Reading Center is the exception. Muslims definitely prefer social assistance to be maximized and Christian witness minimized. That is understandable, from their point of view.

The Philippines is an archipelago of 7,100 islands (at low tide). Scattered throughout the country are beautiful resorts staffed by gracious service personnel. The beaches are some of the best in the world.

Even living in the megalopolis of Manila has some major benefits. Well-stocked department stores are prolific. Malls are huge, some with as many as twelve movie theaters. Almost all American fast food restaurants have staked a gastronomical claim to the Filipinos' eating habits. Many young people prefer a Big Mac or a Shakey's pizza to a rice and fish lunch.

After living in Bangladesh for twenty years, life in the Philippines, overall, is a breeze. When we hear Americans complaining about conditions here, we are tempted to suggest they transfer to a rural area of Bangladesh for a few years.

Chapter 13

A Potpourri of Experiences

Some nine centuries ago, Muslims from Malaysia sailed into the Sulu archipelago to the large island of Mindanao in the Southern Philippines. They came as fishermen and traders. Delighted to find peaceful natives and adequate economic opportunities, many opted to settle down and integrate into the local social structures. This meant taking wives who basically were animistic in religious belief and practice.

Islam is second only to Christianity as a propagating force. Soon, wives, relatives, and neighbors were discarding the overt worship of nature and embracing the Muslim faith. I use the word "overt" in a calculated manner. Yes, the prescribed forms and rituals of Islam, at least nominally, were followed. But, in the dark of night, many continued surreptitiously to slip out to the witch doctor for healing, exorcism, or deliverance from an evil curse.

The contrast between animistic practice and Islamic orthodoxy has caused some concern to Muslim religious leaders down through the centuries. But, basically, there has been accommodation rather than confrontation. Overall, Islam has been satisfied with external observances, without delving deeply into the personal aberrations of one's religious practices. The focus has always been the confession of faith in Allah, and Muhammad as the unique prophet and messenger of God. On the practical level, it seems the worst sin a Muslim can commit is blasphemy against Muhammad.

Therefore, it is best to refer to the religion of the Southern Philippines as "Folk Islam." One evening I was sitting in Cotabato City in Mindanao watching the evening news, when the newscaster began excitedly telling a story about "Miracle Monkey." As he talked, pictures were being shown of scores of white-capped Muslims making their way to a nearby village where a spirit-empowered monkey resided. The story had circulated that an extremely ill child had touched the animal and was instantaneously healed. This inspired the faithful of the community to go on pilgrimage to the pond where the monkey lived and seek supernatural release from their physical ailments. If the monkey could not be touched, it was adequate to offer him bananas. Many Muslims filled bottles with the pond's water which was supposedly energized by the monkey's presence. This water was used as a healing agent by drinking it or by external application to the body. Such is the ongoing reality of folk practices among Muslims in Mindanao.

Throughout the 300 years of Spanish, and 50 years of American Colonial rule, Muslims in Mindanao steadfastly resisted alien control of their lives. Their goal, through negotiation or violence, has always been to maintain maximum political and judicial autonomy over their societal concerns. Areas like allowing them polygamy and divorce have been demanded.

Historically, the ruling powers in the Philippines have used a carrot and stick approach to the "Muslim problem." Over the centuries, negotiations have been the preferred option, but periodically, civil war has raged across the island. In more recent years, there have been intense, formal consultations between Muslim and Government leaders. Concurrently, Islamic radicals have engaged in terrorist acts that have paralyzed normal business activities in certain areas of Mindanao. Robbery, murder, and kidnapping for ransom are common means by which the extremists keep pressing their demands for autonomy.

Most Muslims reside in central or western Mindanao. The majority of the residents on the island are Christian, while only five million are Muslim. During the Marcos presidency, Christians were urged to take up residence in Mindanao. Cheap land was made available to the settlers who were willing to live in close proximity to Muslims. This obvious attempt on the part of the Government to dilute the demographic strength of Muslims has been intensely resented.

Antagonism is a two way street in Mindanao. The majority Catholic and minority Protestant communities are basically obsessed with a fear and hatred of their fellow-countrymen. Many are the warnings given to children by their parents regarding the alleged character defects of Muslims. "The only good Muslim is a dead Muslim," is a saying known to every Christian in the Philippines. Such broad-ranging prejudice is perpetuated generationally. Little effort is extended to make a fair presentation of the positive aspects of Islamic culture. Almost no examples are given of the multitudes of gracious, kind Muslim Filipinos. A large part of the problem lies in the ghettoization of the communities. Few Christians really know Muslims, and vice versa. Thus, a lack of meaningful relationships reinforces negative stereotypes.

There are several well-defined Muslim political organizations that purport to speak for the aspirations of the people. Interestingly, and sadly, these groups often clash with one another on the local provincial level. Jealousy and leadership quarrels lead to violence that leaves many dead and injured in its wake. Unfortunately, there is no lack of high-powered rifles, bombs, and even missiles capable of bringing down hostile fighter planes. These armaments have been supplied from overseas Muslim sources. It would be proper to define the Mindanao situation as a powder keg with a short fuse about to be lit.

Many Christian homes have a loaded rifle hidden away, awaiting the dreaded moment when the Muslims arrive with harmful intent. Though these preparations are defensive in nature, still Christians are not willing to "turn the cheek" in Mindanao. These realities have contributed to the lack of a viable witness flowing from the Evangelical church to the Muslim community.

After thorough consultations following our 1981 survey trip, we decided the most needy area for witness in the Philippines was among the one million Magindanao Muslims. As far as we could research, there was not one convert living out his faith while remaining within his own Muslim extended family and community. Jay Abram, a Christian and Missionary Alliance church planter, had valiantly given witness for over three decades. Prior to his retirement, Jay had seen several Muslims make professions of faith, though, sadly, these converts left their communities and relocated to other areas. They had no ongoing witness to their own people. In total, there are probably less than one hundred pure Magindanao Christians to be found anywhere in the world. The word "pure" refers to the convert having both parents as Muslims, rather than an intermarriage between a Muslim (usually male) and a Christian (usually female).

What an exciting challenge. In 1984, Julie and I moved to the Philippines to initiate the aforementioned outreach to the Muslims of Manila as well as to be a consultant to the emerging team. Within a short time we had 21 adult missionaries on site. They constituted the personnel of the official "Consortium," consisting of three missions: Overseas Missionary Fellowship (OMF), SEND International, and my mission, International Christian Fellowship (ICF, soon to be merged with SIM). Wycliffe Bible Translators (WBT) fielded two couples to commence the huge task of putting the New Testament into a language that would be appropriate for the Magindanao Muslim reader.

To be brutally honest, my vision was intermixed with an unhealthy measure of pride. I had been part of a team that had seen a major evangelistic breakthrough in Bangladesh. I felt it would be relatively easy to guide this flexible, young team into a methodological approach that had already proven itself in one Asian setting. At our quarterly strategy sessions, I was quick to cross-reference every problem with a ready-made solution which had been successful in Bangladesh. Great credit must be given to the Consortium team for their patience and grace in putting up with me during those years.

The struggles and results of the next nine years of Consortium life are documented in chapter 15. None of us ever expected that the battle would be so devastatingly intense. Perhaps there are lessons to be learned from our failures that can be helpful to other teams just entering into the fray of Muslim evangelism.

Perspectives

I have been thinking about perspectives and how a young Muslim man has impacted my life.

Perspective Number 1:

My struggle is to hate the sin (no problem) and yet love the sinner (a gargantuan undertaking). All of this conflict (from my perspective) evolves as a result of a Muslim who is a terrorist, extortionist, fundamentalist, and big time loser in life. From this last sentence you can begin to get the flavor of my myopic vision on the subject.

It happened like this. I was sitting calmly behind the literature table on the sidewalk in front of our Reading Center where the *Jesus* film was being shown in a Muslim language. Suddenly, Datu, the Muslim extremist appeared, in a most agitated state. This was the same guy who had been threatening us for over a year demanding that we close down or be blown up.

Datu began screaming and demanding the equivalent of $25. Upon hearing my refusal he went more than a little berserk and yelled out two phrases repeatedly. One was a gross obscenity and the other was, "I'll kill you." While raging, he pointed his finger about an inch from my nose. In my years living among Muslims I have never been threatened in such a manner.

A friendly and gracious Muslim security guard from next door sought to pacify Datu and bravely stood with me. He had seen a bulge in Datu's back pocket and assumed it was a knife or a gun. I decided I would close down (about ten minutes early). He finally walked off, yelling out his vulgarities and threats.

Perspective Number 2:

Gene Lara, my Filipino colleague, has attempted to help Datu financially. He visited his tiny, dark, airless room that is shared with Datu's eight-month-pregnant wife along with other Muslims. The sweet wife immediately agreed to make some braided bracelets as part of an income generating scheme. We tend to think Datu, for his sporadic "employment," delivers drugs across town for $12 a trip.

Now, what kind of perspective on life can we suggest that Datu may have? First, he was born into violence and confrontation. From childhood he has learned to hate the "Christians" of the Philippines who have denied his people their land and political rights. His response, at an early age, was to join a terrorist Muslim organization.

Secondly, he lives in extreme poverty among filth, squalor, lawlessness, and drugs. His small, crowded room in the Islamic Center breeds friction and restlessness. Being without a job creates low self-esteem. Hunger stalks the 10' by 10' roomful of depressed Muslims. A pregnant wife causes unabated concern. What is to be the future for his unborn child?

Thirdly, a nearby "rich" foreign evangelist with an "extravagant" ten-year-old Toyota car, who propagates a "false" religion, provides a release of sorts for pent up frustration and anger. Demand, Extort, Threaten, Accuse.... Yes, let it boil over. Release, of a sort. Hatred can be an emotional catharsis. The venom that spills forth can be more healing than allowing the rage to simmer and destroy from within.

Perspective Number 3:

The Apostle Paul. Somehow, he empathetically interacted with his opposers. Their community, religion, friendships, and even employment were threatened. Beat him, deprive him, jail him... came forth in a jarring cacophony of sounds, all intended to intimidate and silence this lonely man of God.

And yet, he preached; and yet, he loved; and yet he remained faithful to his last breath. Oh, that I might follow in the train of one eminently qualified to by my exemplar. And, for me, that means I am to love "Sinner Datu," in spite of all that is naturally repugnant to me.

Ayesha

In Manila on a pleasantly cool afternoon, Gerry Aquino, my colleague in ministry, was sitting with me behind our tables of literature on the sidewalk in front of our Reading Center.

A few feet away, the *Jesus* film video played on, seeking to penetrate and thus dispel the spiritual darkness of the small crowd of

Muslims who were attentively listening to a message which could cost them everything, but also give them wealth beyond measure.

Nameless, anonymous, and scorned by a world that measures success by beauty, brains, and brawn, let's call her Ayesha, probably the Muslim world's most utilized female name.

She was perhaps six years old, dressed somewhat shabbily. Her young mother wore the ubiquitous and required hijab (veil) identifying her as a daughter of Ishmail. Ayesha's face was a study in character, history, pain, and fear. There was such a pensive depth in the slight soft brown wrinkle that creased across her forehead. Eyes flashed about, registering apprehension. Her face somehow immediately assaulted my senses.

Slowly, my eyes dropped down over her slight body. Her clothes were soiled and ragged. Then, shock! Ayesha's legs were deformed, spindly, and at wrongly calibrated angles. But the feet, there were no feet! Only stumps. No shoes, only taut, calloused flesh covering leg bones.

Mesmerized, I watched little Ayesha go into the Center with her Mom. They sat on the provided stools and began to watch the *Isa* (Jesus) on the screen as he healed the demoniac and made the blind man to see. I wondered what flitted through the mind of this precious child.

Three times she came out. She hobbled grotesquely down the sidewalk, opened a garbage bag, and deposited her orange peelings. Shyly, she glanced at me with a mixture of bewilderment and fear in her weary eyes. I tried to talk with her, giving her my best American smile of warmth. She was totally unsure of my persona and intent.

Finally, the film was over. I cautiously approached little Ayesha and said, "How are you?" in Tagalog. She leaped away from me and grabbed for the security of her Mom's skirt... refuge, safety, and an insulation from all harm. Mom patted her shoulders in an automatic and oft-rehearsed gesture of assurance that conveyed warmth and unconditional love.

Soon they walked away. I can still vividly see in my mind's eye the bare flesh rhythmically, but not in good sync, pounding down on the harsh pavement of life. What does the future hold for this precious "created in the image of God" Muslim child? What jarring, spiteful words will she have to endure from her peers? Who will want to enter into a marital relationship with a cripple?

Is there hope? Spiritual ... or Physical... or Emotional?

"Thank you, Ayesha, for coming into my life. Thank you for not letting me get hardened to the sufferings of the precious, innocent ones of this indifferent, confused, sin-wracked world in which I live. Thank you for causing me to renew my commitment to be a light in the darkness of Inner-city Manila, even when my flagging flesh has been tempted to rationalize a 'call' to greener pastures."

And, so I press on. "Thank you also, Lord. Thank you for grace to persevere."

Travel

Indonesia: 1984 Irian Jaya, Indonesia. I had been invited to give a seminar to forty missionaries from ten different missions. Dick Corley of International Missions shared the teaching load with me. God has wonderfully visited the highlands of Irian Jaya. The great majority of the former headhunters and cannibals are now believers in Christ.

But in a massive effort to reduce the crowded population in Java, the Indonesian government had undertaken a transmigration scheme to move people southeast to Irian Jaya. Most of these migrants are Muslims. My seminar was an effort to prepare the missionaries to meet this new challenge.

From the port city of Jayapura, we flew over an indescribably beautiful terrain of jungle, swamps, snake-like rivers, and majestic mountains. We came in through a valley and landed on a grass strip 4,000 feet in elevation. As we disembarked, we were surrounded by men wearing only gourds, which covered their genitals, and women clothed with nothing more than grass skirts starting at about bikini level and proceeding downward to just above the knees. Everyone was so uninhibited that soon one forgot the people were in such a state of undress.

The week went splendidly. The delegates were most responsive. A special committee was formed to coordinate a future outreach to Muslims.

Bob and Joyce Sterner are Wycliffe missionaries who are supported by our home church in Detroit. We have been good friends for decades. In 1984, they were missionaries in Irian Jaya, so I decided to visit their remote station. I boarded a small Cessna plane and flew for an hour to the strip at Sarmi where Bob and Joyce were awaiting my arrival. After warm greetings, we forded a river with water up to our waists and then walked three miles along the lovely beach to their home. They were living as simply as any missionaries I have ever met. Their two-room bamboo house had no electricity or kerosene refrigerator, and it was hot! For toilet facilities they had a plastic bucket with a toilet seat on top of it. It was conveniently located right next to the guest bed. Bob emptied it each night in the ocean. Joyce made a two-mile trip to the market at 5 AM three mornings a week.

The Sterners had integrated into a family clan. It was terrific to see the relationship that had been formed. For three months prior to my visit they had stayed in that village without a break. I couldn't help but be humbled by their dedication.

The next morning we started out at 6 AM for the walk to the airstrip. In rather threatening weather, we took off toward Jayapura in the Cessna. About thirty minutes out, we got socked in with clouds and rain. We were flying very low, seeking to get below the bad weather. Several times we diverted. At one point we seemed to be boxed in with solid rain ahead. Suddenly, the pilot did a 180 degree turn and scurried out in search of holes in the clouds. We finally found our valley, slipped down beneath tree level on nearby mountains, and landed safely with little fuel to spare. My very competent Wycliffe pilot friend had two comments: "Praise the Lord" and "It's this type of experience that gives one a few extra gray hairs!" I couldn't help but agree with both statements. What tremendous gratitude I have for these pilots who put their lives on the line for the Gospel.

China: 1985 It was Sunday at 9:30 AM in a hotel room in mid-western China. We placed the blaring television set in the bathroom very near the door which led into the hall where an employee informant of the hotel sat. Over a period of fifteen minutes, the ten members of our Christian tour group casually walked into the room. At the appointed moment, the door opened and in walked a strong, dynamic pastor who belonged to the "underground church." For the next 30 minutes, I had the unique privilege of literally sitting at the feet of a great man of God who had spent 20 years in a horrible Chinese prison, undergoing terrible deprivation and humiliation—all for his faith in Christ. His message, powerful even through interpretation and interspersed with songs, contained such gems as: "This is our Babylon, but our heart is in Jerusalem;" "Satan attacks believers with sweetness and ease as well as with the force of a roaring lion;" "We as Christians often have a mist over our hearts;" and "We must walk with God from Bethlehem to Golgotha."

In such a humble spirit, he spoke of the intense pressures to deny Christ. He said, "I may be a Peter, but I'm not a Judas." Often, he would point to his knees and exhort us to pray with renewed fervency for a spread of revival in China. He lived in a one-room shack on the outskirts of town and each day worked on a construction gang. But at night, and on Sundays, he was uniquely active for the Kingdom. The week before we met him, he had baptized one hundred new believers.

Such was just one of a number of special occasions when we met with Christians who were peasants, intellectuals, students, and professionals. One dear, old great grandmother, who was a medical doctor, told of going to the park daily to share her faith. Her goal was to win one person to Christ each day. During the Cultural Revolution, she was demoted from her position as head of obstetrics at a hospital and made to do the work of an orderly emptying bedpans. But what a sweet spirit! Another official high in the government told of God's sustaining power over the past four decades. He had an unbelievably overt witness for Christ. A young professional, new in the faith, told of reading four chapters in the Word each night after her three roommates had gone to bed. We also met an American couple who teach English in a university. At Christmas and Easter they had had tremendous opportunities to share

Christ with faculty and students. Christmas decorations were still up in the faculty lounge in May!

How simply the people lived. Most workers received $25 per month. Rent and food were cheap, but it took three months' wages to purchase a bicycle. The two 8 foot by 10 foot rooms that families lived in were dingy and barely adequate. Bath facilities were limited to a washbowl in the living room! The unheated public toilet for all to use was 50 yards down the street. Can you imagine making that trip several times a day in sub-freezing winter months?

Yet, there was a fantastic ethos of excitement in China. Free enterprise markets packed out the sidewalks each night, selling everything from furniture to live chickens. At least half the population had discarded the drab gray uniforms to wear bright, attractive pants and skirts. Small television sets were to be found in thousands of homes. Shadow boxing exercises were done in the early morning hours out on the streets to the accompaniment of Kenny Rogers blaring out of pocket radios! The absence of children was astonishing. One child per family was the norm.

How friendly the people were. On the streets we were frequently approached by gracious Chinese wanting to practice their English. The constant refrain was, "Now the Chinese and Americans are friends." We encountered no restrictions. Even on the Christian scene, the government had allowed 1½ million Bibles to be printed in the country in just five years. In Shanghai, over 3,000 gathered to worship each Sunday morning in just one church. How exciting.

Auschwitz: 1987 For most of my life, I have struggled with the reality of the Holocaust. How could it ever have happened? Under emotional, spiritual, and intellectual compulsion, Julie and I journeyed back through history and experienced but a small portion of that horrible encounter between Gentile and Jew. The following was written shortly after we completed our visit to Auschwitz, Poland.

* * *

On a cold, wet, and dreary Sunday morning, Julie and I were walking along a Warsaw street when we noted a steady stream of people making their way into a church. We joined the Poles as they crowded through a small door and sat on plain, high-backed benches. Positioning ourselves in the rear, we observed the congregation of a hundred middle-aged or older men and women as they devoutly worshipped our Lord. An overhead projector provided the words for the songs which were led by the beautiful voice of an unseen young woman. No Bibles or hymn books were in evidence among the worshipers.

As we sat musing in the very back of the church, we were deeply impressed with the obvious sincerity of this band of believers who live under a repressive Communist system of government. Since 1939, the Poles have groaned under one form of yoke or another. My eyes glanced up toward a commemorative plaque on the wall. Etched into memory and bronze were the names of 30 members of the congregation who had personally fueled the furnaces of Hitler's madness. Some were in their 20's, and others beyond 50. Beside their name was listed the dreaded camp in which each died. Auschwitz was the fiery host to over half of the patriots.

As I reflected, the congregation began to softly sing, "I surrender All." The pews seemed to come alive with a sense of collective history. Persecution, pain, and perplexity experienced under the devastating influences of Nazism and Communism had not succeeded in denting the faith of the Poles. In contrast, secularism and materialism have neutralized the Church in Western Europe where highly prized democratic values have evolved into a sensuous orgy of narcissism and hedonism. How terribly sad.

We left the church and somberly retraced the boundaries of the infamous Warsaw Ghetto. Thousands of Jews, declared guilty of an unclean birth, had been herded together into a *cordon sanitaire*. To the astonishment of the Nazis, these unworthy specimens of humanity staged a massive but futile last gasp of resistance. They died in pride.

On the plane to Krakow, I finished reading the classic book, *Triblinka*, which tells of another death camp in the north of Poland where hundred of thousands of Jews were gassed. But on August 2, 1943, those remaining "offscouring of the world" staged a revolt that will forever be etched in the annals of history. In an unprecedented act, one thousand starved Jewish prisoners broke into the armory and took possession of guns, hand grenades, and petrol. Within one hour, the camp was burned to the ground and six hundred Jews had fled to the forest. For those brave men, their moment of destiny had been dramatically altered. However, only forty of these men survived until the end of the war.

It is now just a few hours since Julie and I boarded a "tour bus" in Krakow and journeyed for 90 minutes through the lovely Polish countryside. Soon the infamous rail line came into view. The very efficient Nazis had strategically located the Auschwitz camp at a rail junction at dead center of their killing empire. Within a few minutes, we were standing in front of the awesome gate that welcomed four million newcomers into the pit of hell. With a minimum of effort, one could conjecture visions of the moment of eternal decision being made by a Gestapo doctor as he gave temporary reprieve to the healthy. The rest were sent to a large courtyard where they were told to quickly undress and run in the nude to the "showers." Packed into the large room, men, women, and children received not the refreshing cool water to revive their tired, aching bodies, but rather the "coup de grace" of cyanide pellets that sent them propelling into eternity. Within 30 minutes the graveyard shift came in to extract gold from teeth and cut off the women's hair. They then ran with the bodies to the bonfires or to the cremation ovens.

As we walked through the camp, as we surveyed the double fence of electrified barbed wire, as we relived one of man's cruelest and most barbaric moments, we felt emotionally drained and physically nauseated. In the barracks, we saw massive piles of each of the following: shoes, discarded artificial limbs, women's hair (which 45 years later still emitted the smell of poisonous gas), children's clothes, suitcases, prayer shawls, cooking utensils, toothbrushes, and eyeglasses. Photographs, camp documents, mug shots of prisoners, and hundreds of other items of memorabilia filled the rooms.

One of the most devastating areas was the death block where prisoners were either tortured or shot to death. One cell was dedicated to starvation and another to darkness. Yet another was a two foot by two foot, totally enclosed area, that was entered by crawling in through a small opening in the bottom. Four prisoners then stood jammed against each other for the duration of their sentence. The death block barracks contained pathetic messages scribbled on the ceiling by the condemned from the top of their three-tier bunk beds. The final indignity of 20,000 prisoners was to strip and line up against an outside wall and be shot to death.

We walked by the roll call courtyard where prisoners had to stand for up to four hours twice a day. Then, on to the place where the camp orchestra was forced to entertain the emaciated as they went to and from the nearby factories for their ten-hour work day. We saw a representation of the soup and bread that barely kept a soul alive in a skeleton. Then a horrifying look at an intact gas chamber and, conveniently located, adjacent crematorium. The only consolation was the gallows erected nearby where the first commander of Auschwitz was hanged in 1947.

Slowly, we re-entered the bus for a one-mile drive to Birkenau, a large camp built for 200,000 prisoners. We surveyed scores of barracks, huge crematories in the distance, and then the inevitable railway siding with its lingering message of the cruelty of "selection," a euphemism invented by the SS officers.

We drove back to our hotel tonight in the dark. My heart aches as I write these words. No prose, no poetry, no snapshot, no newsreel... no, **nothing** can begin to compare with the reality of visiting, seeing, and reflecting on the unbelievable depths to which man, made in the image of God, can descend.

Tonight we decided to forego our planned meal. We ate instead bread and soup, and let our minds wander back into a very recent moment of history.

* * *

What great opportunities the Lord has given us to see history come alive in our travels during these past decades.

Death

Dad's eccentricities, continuing even after his conversion, perplexed and confounded me. But I was committed to love this man who, genetically and sociologically, played such a major role in my formation as a person.

During visits to Miami on home assignments, I would accompany Dad to his places of interest. One of his only hobbies was to go fishing in the canals at the edge of the Everglades. Dad was an expert at relating grandiose stories about the ones that got away. Seldom did he produce fruit for his labor. I have always considered fishing a profound exercise in futility. One of the few times I accompanied Dad on a trip, I was ticketed for driving the car along at the brisk pace of 79 MPH. The family all accused me of seeking to terminate my excursion as quickly as possible.

As Dad approached 75 years of age, we all counseled him to end his love affair with his dilapidated car. He was 80 percent deaf, with poor eyesight—truly, an accident waiting to happen. Nothing we said put a dent in his total commitment to that which gave him his last vestige of independence. Dad was supremely sovereign during those solitary moments behind the wheel. He was totally in control, answerable to no one. It was unthinkable for him to voluntarily relinquish this one remaining power base of his life.

While I was teaching a module at Biola University in January 1986, I received a phone call from Miami saying the inevitable had happened. In broad daylight, Dad made a left turn in front of an oncoming car driven by an elderly Cuban man. Both men were in the hospital. Dad's condition was life threatening. Julie and I immediately flew to Miami to be at his bedside in the intensive care unit.

In the days that followed, it seemed that Dad would recover. We had good talks and prayer together. The Cuban man had recovered. It was with this optimistic outlook that we left Miami and returned to Manila. Six weeks later we received a call saying Dad had died. My brother Jimmy arranged for Dad's cremation. There was no public service because, apart from the few family members, there was no one who would attend. A sad last chapter to a 75 year pilgrimage on planet earth.

In many ways, I feel I was inadequate for my father. All too often, my focus was on how he had failed me. It was so hard to overcome the negative vibes with which I struggled emotionally. But I did sincerely attempt to do better. I must rest my case with the

Lord who knows my innermost desires as well as my inability to fulfill those desires.

And then there was Mom. There was always an intense anticipation as we came to our times of visiting Miami. For it was there I would be privileged to be in Mom's presence. The mystical bond between Mom and her youngest son was never interrupted or hindered in any way. Her idiosyncrasies were never a bother. I was somehow always overcome with gratitude at how much suffering and hurt she had endured in her lifetime. She never gave up.

Mom loved me in a different sort of way. She hated writing letters, thus my weekly correspondences to her and Dad received minimal replies. Phone calls to us would be too expensive. As an adult, I cannot recall receiving gifts from Mom. There was never any extra money for such things. She did not travel to attend our wedding or to observe my graduation ceremonies from college or graduate schools.

Yet, there was never doubt about the depth of love Mom had for me. I could sense it in her eyes that twinkled when I came into her presence. It was evident when she, as a basically quiet person, would rattle on about inconsequentials as we sat together over a cup of coffee around the kitchen table. Then there was her hug of love as I would say good-bye for yet another four years of separation.

A year after Dad died, word came to us in Manila that Mom had cancer and that it was quickly spreading throughout her body. I made a special trip to the States right after Christmas 1987. So memorable are the events of those few days that we all spent at my brother's house. A fall from bed as Mom tried to get up brought a weakened call of distress, "Phil Jr., Phil Jr." On another day, her request for me to cut her toenails was pathetic and yet endearing.

Then came New Years Eve 1987. My brother sat on the couch on one side of her and I on the other side. The unarticulated thought of the three of us was, "Never again like this, this is the end." I choked back tears as we held hands and prayed in the New Year. The next night I knelt by her bed and gently whispered, "Mom are you absolutely sure you know Jesus as your Savior and that you are ready to go to Heaven?" Back came the unhesitating reply, "Phil Jr., of course, I've told you that before." The next day I returned to Manila.

A week later Mom was put in a nursing home where she could have 24-hour care. She only lived for another month. My sister-in-law told me of a touching scene which occurred just before she died. Mom had been in a coma and suddenly became conscious and alert. She sat up in bed and looked toward the bathroom door and cried out in a voice laced with distress, "No, Phil Jr., don't go through that door, don't leave me, come back, come back."

And thus, the curtain of death descended upon that frail body curled up on an anonymous hospital bed. Rest and peace at last. For me, there yet remains one more glad reunion with Mom, and from that moment on through eternity. No more sad moments of going through the door and no more sounds of a weakened voice crying out, "Don't leave me, come back, come back."

Wedding

For parents of an only child, the experience must be uniformly traumatic. Responsibility descends from Heaven like a smothering blanket. Yes, Dad must, by all means fair or foul, make sure his beloved daughter marries just the perfect specimen of the male race.

Lyndi's "almost never without a boyfriend" style kept her dad busy evaluating and counseling. Finally, it all came together in David Thomas, a "missionary kid" born and raised in the Philippines. David's 6 foot 4 inch frame impressed Lyndi, as did his evident maturity and focus in life. From her 5 foot 2 inch perspective, she would find it easy to look up to David physically. But this was peripheral to the emotional and spiritual qualities she also recognized in him.

So, with acceptance from all sides, the big wedding occurred on August 10, 1991. David's dad, Fred Thomas, conducted the ceremony, while I shared a few thoughts of reflection and exhortation. How good the Lord was to bring David into our family.

Overseas Ministry Study Center (OMSC) and Yale University

A unique opportunity was given to Julie and me in the Fall of 1993. I was asked to be the "Senior Scholar In Residence" at the OMSC in New Haven, Connecticut. This center is an exciting think tank which sponsors weekly seminars and modular courses, which are taught by some of the world's leading missiological experts.

My responsibility for three and a half months was to be a resource person to the thirty missionaries who were in residence in the OMSC apartments. We were provided with a lovely two-bedroom accommodation. I taught one of the courses on the subject of Muslim evangelism. During the semester I spoke at several public meetings and also taught a Sunday class at nearby Black Rock Congregational Church.

OMSC director, Gerry Anderson, arranged for me to apply to Yale University as a "Research Fellow." This led to my acceptance, and the opportunity to audit classes at Yale. Also, I was able to avail myself of the Divinity School's missiological library, perhaps the best in America. I sat in on Lamin Sanneh's class on Islam. Sanneh, as a full professor at Yale, is probably the world's most academic Muslim convert. The day he gave his conversion testimony to us students is forever etched deeply into my memory.

Everyone we met at Yale was extremely nice to us. How surprising to find that five of my books are in the Yale library. As a result of this Fellowship, I am considered an alumnus, and therefore receive the standard financial appeal letters along with the Philippine "Yale Club" invitations to mix with the high and mighty.

Birth

Julie and I had scheduled a heavy program of meetings in the States for the summer of 1995. Then came the announcement of the impending birth of our first grandchild, which a sonogram indicated would be a healthy boy. Much to our disappointment, we had to wait out news of the birth from a motel in Atlanta, Georgia. Los Angeles never seemed so far away.

After hours of painful labor, the doctors decided on a cesarean section. Around 2 AM on June 8, 1995, the much anticipated call came, announcing the successful entry of 9 pound 5½ ounce Ian Philip into the world. He was three weeks old when we finally saw him.

Almost three years later, came the birth of Jacqueline Rose on March 18, 1998. Rose, being Julie's middle name, bestows on her the shared responsibility we both now have of modeling our Lord to our two namesakes.

Chapter 14

Missionaries

At this point, I would like to record some impressions of missionaries I have met throughout my pilgrimage. Both Bangladesh and the Philippines have provided a close-in look at these soldiers of the cross. Also my hours of listening to missionaries during seminars in various countries, as well as in my classes in the West, have given me this basis for reflection. It is safe to say, my most intense joys as well as my greatest shattering of expectations have come from the missionary community.

Let me begin with myself, a case study in sin and sanctification; light and darkness; spiritual success and defeat. How can such an antithesis coexist in one of God's redeemed children? The Apostle Paul seemed to struggle on this same level as he sets forth failure in Romans 7 and Holy Spirit empowerment in Romans 8. Apparently this conflict was ongoing, with total release only being experienced when he was ushered into the presence of the Lord.

My prayer letters have sought to honestly depict personal joys and defeats. By far the letter that produced the most response was the following:

> *The letter I received recently was headed, "Faithful are the wounds of a friend." UH OH, I thought, I'm in for trouble!*

Throughout the remainder of the aerogram, my motivation for ministry was incisively dissected. The basis for my "friend's" evaluation was our news/prayer letter which he had been reading for thirty years. We have only met briefly on two occasions during this time. His correspondence with me has been minimal.

Bob (not his real name), has judged that Pride and Self are major motivators in my service for the Lord. Evidence: (1) the successes, achievements, honors, and opportunities that I have chronicled in some detail within our newsletters over the decades; (2) inadequate attributions to the Lord as the source of my accomplishments that may have taken place in my ministry.

PLEA. Guilty—with explanation. One of the most frustrating things I struggle with in the Christian life is the whole area of motivation. Where is the line drawn that delineates God's glory from Phil's glory? With me, I must start with a premise of an abundance of pride that seems to effectively infiltrate each of my brain cells. I bask in recognition and delight in the satisfaction that follows on from someone, somewhere praising me.

But there immediately follows a real sense of unworthiness and awe that the Lord could use me in any way at all. Deep down there is a cognizance of my total inadequacy and my dependence on Christ, Julie, and a multitude of friends who have made these years of missionary life a reality. So, the intertwining of Self and God continues to assault my innermost being, which in turn creates a murky evaluation of my spiritual status. What to do? Stop writing—it's just an ego trip. Don't teach—it's for self-exaltation. Decline opportunities which lead to positive notoriety—it's all based on the pride of life.

Should I undergo a metamorphosis that could wind me down to a state of inertness? Off to an evangelical monastery! (Is there such a thing?) Oh, the spiritual purity of being a zero. No, I don't see that evolution taking place anytime soon. Therefore, hang in with me as I pilgrimage on

*through a maze of mixed motives. As you are a part of a very
small group of people who receive this letter, feel free to
counsel, rebuke and guide me as I honestly seek to become a
more committed bond slave of Christ. Above all, please, BY
PRAYER, move me closer to this goal in life.*

Most everyone was graciously affirming of me. I especially
appreciated the few who empathized with the struggle and counseled
appropriate vigilance. How helpful have been those who, over the
decades, have humbly pointed out inadequacies in my life. Without a
doubt, these brave souls, who have risked confrontation, have been
used of God to pull me back from the brink of spiritual decline.

In thinking about other missionaries, let me commence with the
positive. Missiological theory has been a major part of my academic
and teaching pilgrimage. But I have never been content with theory
which is untested by the harsh realities of real-life encounters.
Missionary biography has opened a challenging and exciting world
to me. Within these stories one finds the balance between postulation
and performance. One historical example will suffice.

William Carey, the father of modern day missions, went to what
is now Bangladesh at the end of the 18th century. Shortly thereafter,
he shifted his focus to a compound in Serampore near Calcutta where
he remained, without furlough, in selfless ministry for forty years.
His towering accomplishments have been documented elsewhere.
What is not so well known is Carey's struggle with his paranoid
wife, Dorothy. James Beck's *Dorothy Carey* documents this painful
episode which stretched on for what must have seemed an
interminable twelve years.

From arrival in India, Dorothy was in a downward spiral. On the
physical side, she had struggled through seven pregnancies in
fourteen years. Debilitating dysentery was her constant companion.
Added to these infirmities would have been the unceasing struggle
with climate and culture. Having lived for five years without
electricity in near proximity to the Careys' home, I can empathize
with her sense of being overwhelmed.

Without doubt, these realities contributed to the mental
deterioration of Dorothy. By 1796, we have this terribly sad

description of her condition. These words were penned by Carey's missionary colleague, medical doctor John Thomas.

> *Mrs. Carey has given us much trouble and vexation, and has formed such black designs and carried them so far into execution that we have been obliged to go to Heaven for help. Do you know that she has taken it into her head that C(arey) is a great whoremonger; and her jealousy burns like fire unquenchable; and this horrible idea has night and day filled her heart for about 9 or 10 months past; so that if he goes out of his door by day or night, she follows him; and declares in the most solemn manner that she has catched him with his servants, with his friends, with Mrs. Thomas, and that he is guilty every day and every night.... She has uttered the most blasphemous and bitter imprecations against him, when Mrs. Thomas and myself were present, seizing him by the hair of his head, and one time at the breakfast table held up a knife and said, "Curse you. I could cut your throat." She has even made some attempt on his life. And for some minutes together she will say, "You rascal: You d—d rogue! God almighty damn you," etc., etc., too bad to mention and far worse if possible in obscenity than in profaneness. I need not go further to convince you that we have had our troubles. For some ladies have almost hesitated, till, thank God, she accused them of being intimate with her husband and then they understood she was out of her senses. But before it was doubtful. In all other things she talks sensible and she minds nobody nor fears any one but me. If I come into the room and she is raving, she stops. She has been in confinement by my advice. Yet she speaks highly of me as a good man, but deceived in Carey. In this country everything must be known of this sort* [*]*

Can you imagine Carey walking through crowded Indian markets followed by his wife screaming obscenities and accusing him of habitual adultery? For over a decade, the mild-mannered

---

[*] Beck, James R. *Dorothy Carey, The Tragic and Untold Story of Mrs. William Carey.* Grand Rapids, Baker Book House, 1992, p. 109.

Carey endured such totally undeserved vilification. At certain periods, Dorothy had to be physically restrained in her room.

One contemplates such a testing with awe. How could Carey possibly have endured without having a nervous breakdown? By what empowerment was he enabled to continue in his linguistic achievements that produced portions of the Bible in 39 Indian languages? In one nine year period, 31 million pages of the Old and New Testament were printed on his presses. In William Carey we find a model of integrity and perseverance.

More Heroes of the Faith

Others, more contemporary in my "hall of fame," include missionary doctors. Vic Olsen, the afore mentioned surgeon of international repute, ministered in Bangladesh for several decades. It was a privilege to be a friend of Vic's and to entertain him and his wife Joan in our home on many occasions.

I particularly remember one blazing hot day in May when Vic and I were wiping away sweat while trying to cajole a minor government official into performing his assigned task. Looking into the weary face of Vic, I said, "Here we stand mired in frustration and exasperation. You could be a famous surgeon in a modern American hospital. Your research oriented mind would be cranking out postulates for the medical community. Joan and the four kids would be surrounded by suburban affluence. Any regrets?"

Vic, without hesitation, assured me that he was experiencing total fulfillment and satisfaction in his life and career. He humbly downgraded American related professional recognition as compared with the privilege of being an ambassador for the King in Bangladesh. Recently, Vic, at 70 years of age, along with Joan, spent a day with Julie and me in Manila. They were on their way to the States, having just retired from a long and distinguished ministry of servanthood in Bangladesh.

In the mid-80's, I visited the African nation of Niger. What a hostile environment in which to labor. The Sahara Desert relentlessly pushes its mountains of sand further and further southward each year into the heartland of the nation. Dust storms swirl through the villages where veiled and shrouded Muslims acquiesce to the invasion with a shrug and a declaration that all is the will of Allah. Soaring temperatures that exceed 100 degrees Fahrenheit stifle initiative and accomplishment.

Driving through miles of barren landscape, I became convinced this was as close as one could come to the proverbial "God-forsaken land." God does, however, have a significant representation in Niger. Our Landrover, full of weary missionaries, finally arrived at Galmi, a sleepy little village made up of several hundred small mud brick houses and a few shops. In the midst of this drab setting is one of the most acclaimed hospitals in all of Niger.

Dr. Andrew Ng and his wife Belinda, both Singaporeans of vivacious temperament, warmly welcomed us to SIM's mission hospital. Forever etched in my mind is Andrew standing in the midst of a simple ward surrounded by scores of needy Muslims. In all the heat and dust, here was a surgeon willing to forgo the sterile cleanness of Singapore to minister in such a setting.

Years later, Andrew and Belinda were asked to return to Singapore to serve as SIM's East Asia Director (thus becoming my supervisor). As I visited his modest apartment on the 12th floor of a rather unpretentious building, I was again deeply impressed with Andrew's persistent dedication. His open option had been to practice as a surgeon at a salary of $250,000 per year. Instead, he has chosen an income equal to that of the newest SIM missionary with a Bible-school education.

Dr. Phil McDaniel is a missionary medical doctor in Thailand. Both his father and grandfather served in the same capacity in the same country for many years. Julie and I had the privilege of meeting Phil and his wife Melba while we were residents together at the Overseas Ministries Study Center in New Haven, Connecticut. Memorable was one night during a small group meeting when Phil and Melba shared their testimonies about missionary life in a remote area of Thailand adjacent to the infamous bridge over the River Kwai.

After describing their ministry, Phil began to talk about Melody, their eight-year-old daughter. This "special" child is mentally impaired. She cannot be left without supervision. At times, her frustration spills over into anger and from there into embarrassing behavior. Phil and Melba are special models of parenthood as they exercise supernatural patience with Melody.

One illustration Phil shared was particularly powerful. In her early years in Thailand, Melody was not learning how to crawl, much less walk, which would have been normal for her age. Melba realized they might forever have an incapacitated child, one that would not be much more than a human vegetable.

Not willing to assign her precious daughter to such a fate, Melba would get down on the wooden floor of their home and, for hours, crawl back and forth as a teaching tool for Melody. In the searing heat and high humidity, day after day, she would crawl beside Melody while exhorting her to give it a try. Slowly, ever so slowly, Melody began to slide, then crawl, then take her first tentative steps. Today this special child walks and runs with gay abandon.

At any point the McDaniels could have retreated to America where Phil would have been a successful physician. Melody would have been given the best in professional care. Melba's lifestyle would have been a far cry from her daily hassle with life in Thailand. But I do ponder whether anyone but a loving mother crawling on the floor for interminable hours could have taught little Melody how to walk. Such dedication, not only to a daughter, but to a missionary calling is exemplary.

In 1999, I was privileged to minister in one of the most inhospitable countries on the planet. The following is a reflection I wrote concerning those who incarnate their faith and life in such a setting.

> *The pilot announced our imminent landing. With my nose pushed against the plane window I was startled to see only mile upon mile of nothing but the sand dunes of the Sahara Desert. As we came very near the ground I was relieved to see five trees forming an "oasis in the desert." Within seconds we were on the tarmac stirring up clouds of the red, powdery sand of the Sahara that totally permeates the small capital city of this North African 99.9 percent Muslim nation.*

What a challenge to give Bible studies to 35 of God's special frontline evangelistic pioneers. All of the missionaries are under visas that allow them to work within NGO's (non-government organizations). In this manner they can assist Muslims physically. Any evangelism must be done with great care. They live under constant threat of police searches and orders of expulsion.

My first night was spent in a small home shared by missionaries and Muslims. Tim and Sheri with two small children live in two 12' by 12' rooms with no bed or furniture. Mattresses on the floor provide sitting, eating, and sleeping "comfort." They have no electricity, no fans, no refrigerator and no oven. Light is provided by candles. The outhouse squat-type 4' by 4' toilet room is shared with a Muslim family. One takes his or her water bucket into a separate 4' by 4' room for a pour bath. The roof in the two rooms is tin with no ceiling underneath. This couple both have ivy league degrees and Tim is probably the most intellectual missionary I have ever met anywhere. To top off my vignette, this family has lived in these two rooms for 12 years, the last six with kids, whom Sheri home schools. WOW! Who am I to minister to these 35 ambassadors of sacrifice, almost all of whom live similarly to Tim and Sheri?

Light shining into the stygian darkness of an anti-Christian society. Some forty locals have placed their faith in Christ. I was so privileged to minister to 25 of them. Particularly memorable was the night I spoke to 12 of the believers, all of whom had only been Christians between three and nine months. Walking among the first generation of believers in a country held tight in the vise grip of Islam for 1,350 years was almost emotionally more than I could handle.

Couscous and camel meat was a common meal during my stay. I also had my first taste of camel milk. Dates are plentiful and delicious. One early morning a group of us went a few miles out of town and watched the sun rise over the vast ocean of sand dunes. We enjoyed the cool season, but the 120 degree searing heat of April and May is soon to engulf the country. Sand storms frequently blow through the land. Amazing how the foreigners, in that extreme heat, can wear the huge amount of material that constitutes African dress!

One day the Muslim director of all the NGO's came to give greetings to our group. A team member asked him how their people could better identify with the nationals and how they could do a better job. Without hesitation, he looked over at Tim and said, "Just be like him." What a tremendous commendation for a messenger of the Gospel in one of the most hostile settings on planet earth!

Many other positive case studies could be cited, but with space limitations, I share just one more. Ed and Irene Welch, for years, lived in a small town in Bangladesh where they were repeatedly harassed by rowdy children. At any time of the day or night, rocks would come raining down on their roof or land in their courtyard. Kids would climb onto the top of their wall and cause big time irritation to the three Welch children, one of whom responded by commencing a stutter in his speech—which continued for two years. The Welches' patience was rewarded years later when the Southern Baptists took over the work and were enabled to see a number of churches emerge from that once barren and resistant soil.

The Other Side of the Coin

Without any doubt, my overall impression of the missionary community is positive. Yet seldom in this fallen world is anything 100 percent. My negative critique of the foreign missionary falls into three categories: Purity; Productivity; and Perseverance.

Purity In chapter 10, I touched on man's sexual vulnerability. Two missionary illustrations were cited. Here I would like to just add two more disappointments to those already given. Sam, with his wife and small children, was assigned to a church planting ministry in a small town in an Asian country. Results were slow in forthcoming and discouragement began to dominate Sam's life. He was in an emotionally vulnerable state.

There was one exciting dimension to the household. Pamela, the cute and personable live-in house helper was always available for interesting conversations, particularly when Sam's wife was gone with the children to a neighborhood Bible study. Incrementally, the descent from the emotional to the physical took place. One afternoon the line was crossed. Though guilt was a nagging companion for Sam, his compelling sex drive had now completely captivated him. Secret liaisons continued unabated.

They continued, that is, until disclosure was mandated by the discovery of Pamela's pregnancy. The family, mission, church community, and home supporters were all stricken with hurt and disgust. Sam and his family were sent back to their home country. Not long thereafter, Sam divorced his wife. Pamela gave birth to a son who has had to bear an aura of shame for which he was personally faultless. For years the mission assisted financially in his child support.

Daniel was an international missionary with an Asian passport. He was one of my "top of the line" spiritual heroes. Always in great demand as a speaker at large conferences throughout the world, Daniel consistently shared a fresh, deep, challenging word from the Lord. Few were his equal. It was so good to see a humble man of God with such depth who also was graced with a most winsome personality. He was walking proof of the validity of the selfless ministry of the early missionaries who first took the Gospel to his land. I was eagerly looking forward to intimate fellowship with him at a large conference in Asia where we would both be plenary speakers—he for four sessions and I for one.

Then, suddenly, at the last minute the meeting organizers received a letter from Daniel canceling his participation. Soon word was out that upper-middle-aged and married, Daniel had, for many months, been committing adultery with a young, attractive woman. Shock waves rolled through the international evangelical community. How could a Christian who had come so far descend to the depths of deceit and unfaithfulness? At last report, Daniel and his wife remain together while he is being counseled by concerned Christians on a regular basis.

These sad stories, plus others that bombard us through the media, are proof positive that Christian leaders are not in any way immune to the destructive influences of Satan. There is absolutely no one who can feel insulated from potential demonic attack. For men, this is particularly true in regard to sexual purity. Those who have fought the battles and stayed the course are my models and encouragers. Those who have capitulated and gone the easy way of the flesh have devastated me.

Productivity In the July 1990 issue of *Evangelical Missions Quarterly*, I authored an article on the subject of missionary productivity. My thesis was that our community could do much better in making things happen. Our propensity toward an independent orientation to life, coupled with the inadequacy of the average mission's administrative structure, leads to poor accountability. This is not a problem for the highly motivated, innovative, choleric missionary. With or without oversight, he or she is going to be productive. But for the disorganized and laid back person, this can led to stagnation and even regression.

For some, language acquisition is a giant hurdle that bogs the missionary down in a morass of discouragement. Particularly at risk also are missionaries who engage in evangelism among a resistant peoples group. It is extremely difficult to maintain a high level of motivation when one persistently meets with rejection and even scorn.

Not a few missionaries find it easy to rationalize diversions. An amazing cognitive transition has taken place in the brains of many in regard to a simple keyboard. Few were the male missionaries who could be persuaded to sit down in front of a typewriter and get involved in correspondence. Now the same basic keyboard has enjoyed a mystical metamorphous that seduces thousands. Accounts, reports, letters, project proposals, and countless other enticements seem to lure missionaries away from face to face human relationships and place them squarely into a relationship with a faceless cyber space. Add to the above, the temptations to scan the net and to engage in hours of computer games.

Without a doubt, the computer is a fantastic tool, especially for ministries like Bible translation. E-mail is a revolutionary device, saving both time and money. But the diversionary temptations connected with the high tech world need to be admitted and dealt with. I fear this is not being done adequately within our community.

Recreation is a necessary part of missionary life. There is a real danger, however, that a balanced lifestyle can give way to an escapism that is unproductive as well as unhealthy for the missionary's spiritual well being. One new recruit arrived on his assigned field with a drum full of videos! Combine cable TV, a VCR, and a computer, and you have a potentially lethal dose of isolation and even carnality.

Another *Evangelical Missions Quarterly* article that I wrote continues to draw comments twenty years after it first appeared. The title was, "A Small Family Is A Happy Family." This Bangladesh slogan for promoting birth control provided the springboard for my most controversial missiological proposal. I simply made a pragmatic case for missionaries to limit their families to two children. Issues like support, logistics, schooling, illness potential, etc. were mentioned, with a conclusion that I have observed few large families remain on the mission field for an extended period. I shared our testimony of purposefully limiting ourselves to one child because of the nature of the pioneer outreach we would be engaged in. I did make it clear I do not recommend couples to have less than two kids.

It is easy to imagine the defensive reaction of those with four or five children. Examples were cited of large families whose kids returned to the field as missionaries. Without denying such realities, I am forced to compare that number with the withdrawals connected in one way or another to children's concerns. Overall, I stand by my thesis and await statistical proof to convince me otherwise. Incidentally, just to make sure I do not become overly dogmatic, the Lord arranged for our daughter to marry an MK who has four siblings and whose parents ministered in the Philippines in excess of 30 years!

One final concern regarding productivity needs to be voiced. This has to do with careful, calculated, risk-taking. To always be safe can lead to stagnation. Innovation almost always takes the individual beyond the line of total safety. I love the saying, "A ship in a harbor is safe, but that is not what ships are built for."

Over the years, our ship has, at times, been tossed about in turbulent seas. Interestingly, the most severe criticism has not come from non–Christians, but rather from well-meaning, godly believers. They have felt deeply and strongly that I have gone too far in innovation and missiological experimentation. By a process of extrapolation, they have foreseen heresy emerging from my efforts to promote a contextual form of Muslim evangelism.

It is good to be critiqued. Accountability is an imperative part of my life. My writings and ministry have been made stronger by those who have pointed out inadequacies. My only concern is for ministers of the Gospel who tend to only see the dangers and problems. Their lives become deeply mired in a quagmire of conservative complacency. Productivity is thwarted by a fixation on failure potential. I can only cite the Apostle Paul as my model of a risk-taking pioneer. His achievements speak for themselves.

And, thirdly, one final area of concern as relates to missionaries.

Perseverance Why do so few finish the race triumphantly? One of the most frustrating aspects of missiological research is to try to figure out why missionaries leave their field of service. Frequently there is a subtle, unspoken agreement between missionary and mission board, set in motion by the desire of all concerned to save face. How often have you read a prayer letter saying X missionary is leaving the field because of misplaced affections, relational conflicts, or deep depression? More often the reasons given relate to physical illness, children's schooling, or needs of aging parents. Rationalization for such a shading of truth is given by pointing out that there is usually more than one contributing factor to withdrawal. It looks better for all concerned to emphasize certain issues while de-emphasizing others. The end result is that the reasons for our attrition curve are shrouded in an indecipherable fog. Therefore, it is difficult to take corrective action.

But I am drawn to the bottom line. I stand appalled at how many of God's special children arrive on the field full of vision and brimming with new ideas and then within, at maximum, one term have thrown in the towel. Has our culture so conditioned our young people to expect and demand immediate results? What happens when they hit the harsh realities of a baffling language, unfathomable culture, and antagonism to the Gospel message? Is it at this point they emotionally and spiritually collapse? I am afraid that is exactly what happens to many.

There must be new efforts on the part of the church, the theological training facility, and the mission society to overcome these problems. We must, on the field end, begin to welcome not perfect saints, but those committed to endure through blood, sweat, toil, and tears in order to achieve God's salvation for the lost in the unreached nations of the world. It simply cannot be our Lord's best for so many to fall in defeat after so short a time.

To summarize, yes, there are inadequacies and failures in our community. But how overwhelming to see our Lord take unpretentious clay pots which are so fragile and fill them with the water of life. And then miraculously cause that water to be disseminated among the parched and needy.

Chapter 15

Adversity

So much has been written during the past 15 years on the subject of trials. A number of the books ring rather hollow, as if the authors are reporting on a raging war from the comfort zone of a seaside resort. Other writers have marched into Hell, fought valiantly, and emerged scarred but not broken. It is to these sensitive recorders of God's dealing with us in the crucible of adversity that I pay highest tribute.

What have I to add to all of the theological insights of the pundits? Have they not already plumbed the mysteries of God and given us the best possible rationale for allowing the fierce buffeting our souls experience from time to time? Probably so. My small contribution to this subject centers in just the sharing of very personal experiences that will further open a small window on how an inadequate pilgrim comes to grips with the inscrutable ways of a sovereign God. Not always victoriously, certainly not consistently flooded with peace, yet, by His grace, hanging in with tenacity!

Throughout this book, I have already dealt reflectively with this theme. But in this chapter I want to bring together some of the happenings of more recent years. These experiences have been a powerful force in my current spiritual pilgrimage.

Divine Threads Within A Human Tapestry

April, 1985

The headline of the morning paper was crisp and to the point: "Four missing—Six injured—One thousand homes razed—One million dollar loss in shanty town fire."

Such a revelation of tragedy usually calls for a 30-40 second pronouncement of sympathy. This fire was different. It occurred less than half a mile from our home. Billowing orange flames lit up the night sky for hours on end.

I had often driven by this area called *Nazareth* and wondered what it would be like to live as a family of ten in an eight foot by ten foot room bounded by quarter-inch plywood walls and a leaky tin roof. How could one's nervous system accommodate itself to the constant clamor of children, the incessant barking of dogs, the sorrowful weeping of an abused wife, the strain of potential thievery of one's hard-earned pesos, and the heartache of explaining to hungry children that dad had just gambled away his day-laborer salary at the nearby cockfight?

Now, such mundane tragedy paled into insignificance as Julie and I stood for two hours on the abyss of Hades and watched the flames leap from one vulnerable shack to another. Confusion reigned as Filipinos rushed out into the clogged adjacent highway and deposited whatever of their possessions they could salvage from the onrushing torrent of insatiable flames. A mother pensively sat in the middle of chaos and nursed her trusting infant. Nearby, a young man rested his head on a huge generator he had helped pull from one of the nearby shops. Every few minutes he opened his red, swollen eyes to check out his proximity to the flames. A cute thirteen-year-old girl, neatly dressed in her school uniform, was left to guard her parents' few belongings which had been dumped on the road. She continued staring at me with a bewildered look of deep pain. It was as if she wondered what it would be like to be me. Comparatively rich; well dressed; comfortably housed; loving relationships. I stared back at her with an equally bewildered look of deep pain.

Scores of statues of Jesus and pictures of Mary were carried out of *Nazareth* with the same loving care as the family's most prized possessions. Yes, God must be protected from the inferno. But what about God protecting the innocent poor from the fire? I looked up into the clear sky and could only think of one word—rain. "God of the heavens and of nature, please send a cloudburst of unimaginable intensity. Rebuke and dispel the fires of hell." Through the smoke the beautiful, ever so distant stars winked in a mockery of cosmic silence.

The next morning, I quietly shaved in painful reflection while downstairs the Christian radio station played the refrain over and over and over again...

"He's got it all under control,

He's got it all under control,

He's got it all under control."

Such is the paradox the sensitive Christian encounters in active dialogue with the imponderables of life.

July, 1986

A brief foray into Hell: It is just 20 minutes away from the opulence and grandeur of ex-President Marcos' palace. But Hell is light years distant from Imelda Marcos' fairyland of three thousand pairs of shoes, 500 bras, and several full-length mink coats.

Hell is entered by traversing 30 feet along a muddy path which opens into a labyrinth of narrow corridors tightly bordered by wooden shanties. One suddenly realizes he is walking on a sea of compressed garbage which has been discarded by Manila's ten million residents. Karma to some, bad luck to others, and God's sovereign plan of predestination to the more religiously inclined... these are the rationale advanced to explain why some are favored to be born in Malacañang Palace while others are destined to intake their first gasp of noxious air in Hell... more commonly known as the Tondo Garbage Dump... or colloquially referred to as "Smoky Mountain."

As soon as Julie and I rounded the corner, we could see, off in the distance, 25-foot-high mounds of refuse with torrents of dark blue smoke billowing forth from fissures that cut across the three-quarter mile square plot. We were told that internal combustion sparks the flames which produce the smoke which in turn blackens and destroys the lungs of the 800 families who live on the dump. Our "tour" took place on one of the warmer (96°F) Manila mornings. Sweat poured down our faces as we pushed through the smoke, being most ungrateful for the wind which was pushing the blasting hot air off the mountains of burning garbage straight into a community of 5,000 dirty, coughing, ill-clothed, malnourished Filipinos who are commonly referred to rather disparagingly as scavengers.

Just down the lane, we had the privilege of unexpectedly meeting God's special messengers of mercy. Jeremiah, a sharp Filipino working with Youth With a Mission (YWAM), warmly greeted us. In his hand was a large bucket of porridge, which he was distributing to small children who were suffering from malnutrition With him were teams of foreigners who were giving medical aid to the sick and sharing instruction in health care, as well as taking time to just be friends with hurting people.

Yes, these people; people with no claim to laugh or to play or to dance. Yet, there they were gleefully calling out, "Hi, Joe;" children and adults deeply engrossed in a most competitive game of Bingo; a pretty girl managing a small store, overlooking a decorated 10 foot by 20 foot area which becomes the community's dirt dance floor once a week; a teenager lying in his tiny room engrossed in watching one of only two or three TV sets in the dump area; a man just released from prison who now attends a weekly YWAM Bible study; a little girl, almost obscured from sight by smoke, crying, ever so alone in the middle of one of the garbage heaps; the small baby in a hammock who had almost been killed by her father who held her responsible for the death of his wife due to childbirth complications; an old man tattooed from head to toe who throws down his refuse-gathering basket and just silently shakes his head while wiping his profusely sweating brow; and oh, so many little hands reaching out to be held, affirmed, and loved. One little girl just hugged and hugged my legs as though I were her most precious doll.

I asked Jeremiah why his teams went to the trouble of distributing food house to house in all that squalor and disease. Would it not be more efficient to have the people come to a central feeding station? It was a question packed with Western worldview, but was countered by a genuinely sensitive Eastern response. He said it was important to get to know the people personally and intimately if they are to be effective in Christian witness. This could best be accomplished by the casual interaction that takes place in daily house visitation. So, once again, efficient Western methodology is supplanted by a more Christian response to a group of hurting and needy people.

Soon, it was time to walk through the corridor of smoke and over the piles of condensed garbage to the area in "Smoky Mountain" where the trucks unload their daily treasure. The tools of the scavenger trade are a "poking stick" and a four foot high wicker basket. Each truck is greeted with lively enthusiasm. A great crowd gathers to commence poking, probing, evaluating, discarding, and retaining. Jeremiah, once followed an elderly woman scavenger through her day's work. She couldn't competitively push and shove with the younger and stronger. Her turf for gleaning was the peripheral area. At noon, she took a break and for nourishment ordered a piece of bread and half a cup of coffee. At the end of the day she sold her bottles and odds and ends to the appropriate middleman for the paltry sum of forty cents.

Slowly and reflectively, we returned to our Toyota, which to any of our new found friends represents a wealth relative to that of a Marcos Palace. Arriving home, I took a bath, changed my stinking clothes, shined my muddy shoes, and sat down to a more than adequate lunch. And then I tried to pull it all together.

♦ But by the grace of God, I would have been born in that representation of hell on earth. Yet, what about God's grace and those who were born there?

♦ How can they ever, ever laugh and dance? I get grumpy over a piece of burned toast. Who is teaching whom?

♦ A little touch, a squeeze, and a smiling "Hi." How hungry they were for the warmth of human love. But who wants to walk the corridors of hell to share love?

♦ And then there's Jeremiah. A young married man with excellent English and a keen mind. He has voluntarily buried himself in a garbage dump, for the glory of God. "Great, oh, so great in the Kingdom of Heaven."

So we took a brief foray into hell. And the exciting thing is that, in the faces of many outcast scavengers as well as in the godly composure of Jeremiah and other YWAMers, we found heaven!

July, 1990

July 16, 4:26 PM. Our upstairs bedroom-cum-office slowly began a methodical, almost mystical dance in cadence to an unseen driving force. The tempo became faster and more intense. Hundreds of books on the shelves furiously clapped their bodies together. In a frenzy, our cassette player leaped into space. Planks of lumber along the walls awakened from a thirty-year slumber and began loudly to creak and groan in protest to being made to participate in the cosmic ballet.

Subdued fear, not panic, was my reaction as I staggered around the floor, trying to catch the beat and get in step with the orchestrated movement of the universe. The classical music softly playing in the background abruptly shut down—thus registering its disapproval of the harsh sound of rock and roll now intruding into the air waves.

The earth became a gigantic, angry, surging dance hall. Children, high rises, vehicles, the stalks of rice growing in the fields, they all were the dancers. They responded, each in its own way:

♦ Screams filled the air as four stories of a school building pancaked downwards, killing a hundred kids who, seconds before, had been respectfully listening to their teachers.

♦ The Hyatt Terraces, a luxury high-rise hotel in Baguio, built architecturally as a rice terrace, came crashing to the earth in fashion as one domino crashes into its neighbor, thus causing it to join its embrace of death.

♦ A bus driver with his load of precious human cargo slowly winds his way up the steep mountain road... until suddenly there is no road, only the wild abandon of his vehicle tumbling ever downward through the vacuum of space.

Forty-five seconds later, the tumult of the underworld abruptly ends. Hearts pound feverishly; dust rises as on a Hiroshima morning; the surging sea slowly settles. The God of the universal dance has spoken.

Tragedy had once again struck deeply into the heartland of the Philippines. Our area of Manila registered seven on the Richter scale. The mountain resort of Baguio was most severely hit. The multitude, in shock and despair, reflected on the awesome power of an awesome God.

June, 1991

Never has the death of anyone so affected me as has the despicable murder of 33-year-old John Speers. I had bonded so very deeply with John and his lovely family for the 18 months prior to his being killed. The following is what I recorded shortly after John was translated in the presence of our Lord.

> *"John Speers has just been shot in the back of the head and is dead." These incredible words came to me on the phone in our Detroit apartment just three hours after John was murdered by a Muslim who was probably high on drugs. Within two hectic hours, I was on the expressway heading toward the airport to fly back to Manila. John had been with his family in Mindanao for a concentrated month of language study when this senseless tragedy occurred. It seemed simply to have been a "thrill killing" without political or religious motivation.*
>
> *For ten days, I sought to minister comfort to Brenda and to her family who flew out, and to their innumerable friends. At the funeral I shared this eulogy, which I had written on the menu of Northwest Airlines as I flew towards Manila.*

In Memory of John Speers,
Murdered on June 11, 1991,
and to His Wife Brenda,
daughter Shannah (4), and son Josiah (1)

"John, my beloved brother,

"Here I sit on a 747 winging my way to Manila to sit and weep with Brenda, Shannah, and Josiah. Just nine hours ago, at 5 PM on June 11, a sick Muslim Filipino walked up behind you and put a bullet through your brain. Within a very brief time, you put off this garment of temporary flesh and were translated into the presence of the Lord you so dearly loved.

"John, do you remember days we can never retrieve? Like that stormy morning in 1986 in Manila when you braved three-foot-deep floods to get Brenda to the Hospital? A few hours later you ever so joyfully appeared at our front door to proudly announce the birth of Shannah. We hugged and shouted our delight.

"Fast speed to December of '89. It was hard to believe your telephone call. After a tremendously successful first term in Manila helping plant a great church, you were proposing a second term dedicated to working as co-laborers with Julie and me in evangelizing Muslims. Was I ever excited!

"And then you joined us in February of '90. I was quite apprehensive concerning options for your housing in the Muslim squatter section of suburban Manila. But, true to the sterling reputation of you and Brenda, you both immediately accepted a small house with grossly inadequate electricity and non-existent running water.

"What an overwhelming privilege to have put in our time together on the streets of Manila as we gave witness to Muslims. Our long talks on suffering and evil have drawn to a close. John, you now have all the answers. I struggle on....

"You have finished your course in a brilliant flash of victory. Few I have known have loved family, friends, and the lost as you have. Your ministry was always with a definitive focus. Your last walk on earth was down a dusty road in Cotabato City seeking out Muslims who would assist you in learning their language.

"Well, John, all the plans and aspirations we talked of will no longer come to pass. No need to worry about a level 3 in language by January. Future study plans at Wheaton are no longer necessary. You are now more informed than all the Ph.D.'s put together who are yet on this earth.

"Good-bye, John, until the morning comes. I have lost you as one of my closest, most intelligent, and most spiritual friends and will miss you terribly... but only temporarily. I'll see you, in the morning... in the morning."

"Brenda, my dear sister in Christ,

"I will meet you in a few hours. What do I say? It seems like May 18 was but yesterday. Something, or perhaps Someone, compelled Julie and me to go and get you all and take you to the airport. We hugged tightly and I said, "I love you guys." It seemed to have had a deep, emotional impact on me to see you all go off to Mindanao for a month and us off to the States for three months. But, then, what could possibly happen? Nothing final about a three month separation... or could there just possibly be? No, no, not really. Danger of kidnapping, yes, but never murder. No, never.

"And so, the unthinkable becomes a terrible, grotesque reality. Your very, very loving husband, who never ceased to praise you, suddenly becomes a martyr. And you are left with bittersweet memories. Sweet because of the eight years you folded into the embrace of one who regarded you as his beautiful and consistently selfless princess. Sweet because of the constant remembrance of John you have in the heritage of your love outworked in the precious lives of Shannah and Josiah. Bitter because of natural apprehensions at becoming a widow at such a youthful age. Bitter because of missed hugs, and your togetherness dates on Mondays.

"But, Brenda, John's fervent desire for you is to press on in the comfort and peace of Christ. May you somehow be overwhelmed with our Lord's presence.

"You often played and sang so beautifully, 'People Need the Lord.' As that melody and those words wafted from your little, simple home and into neighboring Muslim shanties, your face would intensely convey your love and dedication for those all about you. Love has paid an ultimate price for your dear husband; the supreme test being that of laying down one's life for another.

"You are surrounded by a host of people who love and deeply respect you. We are committed to your support in prayer and care. You know the song 'No more sighing... over there. No more crying... over there. No more dying... over there.' *John beat us to it. And so we sorrow—but not as others who have no hope "*

"Shannah, my precious special friend,

"Oh, how your daddy loved you. One of the high points of his life was to come home each day to your high-pitched, enthusiastic screams, "Daddy, Daddy, Daddy," and then you threw yourself into his arms and just hugged and hugged. You had your dad wrapped around your heart. He just loved to brag about your personality, intelligence, and good looks. What pure unadulterated joy you gave your dad.

"I guess I hurt as much for you and Josiah as I do for your mom. But I am praying and trusting our Lord that you will grow up to be a young lady who so honors her dad by living a life completely dedicated to the Christ for Whom he gave his all.

"I love you very deeply, Shannah. You are unbelievably precious to all of us."

"Josiah, one of the most cuddly boys on earth,

"No, Josiah, you can't really understand; not yet. But you have a dad you can forever be proud of. And your dad was so proud of you as well. He was frequently commenting on how warm and loving you had become. Your eyes would totally light up when dad came home. As soon as big sister got her hugs, you just fell into dad's arms.

"Now, you have a BIG name to live up to: Josiah *the righteous king, and* Speers *the father who so loved that he gave his life.*

"May our Lord enable you and be very special to you."

"To our very dedicated team in the province of Magindanao,

"For years, you have endured the howling winds of adversity. It seems as though there has never been a let-up.

"The world looks on and says, 'You fools, what misplaced allegiance, what loss for naught.'

"And yet, the world was willing to risk thousands of soldiers returning in body bags as a result of engaging in a war for oil. No price seems too high for political or material ends.

"Ours is a war of a different nature. No promotions, no great acclaim, no parades to the cheers of 3 million in New York City. Conversely, we are known as the offscouring of the world.

"But, our march is to that of a different drummer. 'He who loses his life for my sake shall find it.' *Or, as Jim Elliot so eloquently put it,* 'He is no fool to give what he cannot keep in order to gain what he cannot lose.'

"One of our dearly beloved comrades has fallen. We grieve, we hurt, we weep.

"But we do not retreat to safe havens. Our spiritual goals press us forth into danger zones. We take our casualties, not lightly, not frivolously. With sober calculation, we count the cost to family and colleagues.

"But press on we must! With courage, vision, and zeal befitting the memory of our brother in the faith, we must recommit ourselves to the great task of sharing spiritual realities with the Muslims of Magindanao."

"To the murderer of John Speers,

"It is unlikely you will read these words. So perhaps my thoughts are simply a catharsis for my own soul. My mind is totally unable to comprehend you. How could you have killed my brother? You knew him not. He had never offended you. You did not know Brenda, but you have caused her to become a widow. Shannah and Josiah, you have never met, but you have recreated them in a fatherless image.

"Do we belong to the same human family? Can I fathom the hurts and failures that plunged the sword of hate deep into your psyche?

"Here, we are talking about degrees. We all stand guilty before God. There is none righteous, no not one. The ongoing effects of the Fall are cataclysmic. Jesus indicates everyone who hates is a murderer. Therefore we are all indicted.

"I can only commit you to our loving God. May you be released from the stygian darkness of your broken soul. In Christ alone can there be forgiveness and restoration."

"And to all of us who so loved John,

"May God grant us His peace in this tumultuous and hurting hour."

October, 1991

My initial encounter with the surging anger of Mount Pinatubo commenced on the balmy afternoon of June 15. Interrupting our mini-furlough, I had flown back to Manila to participate in the funeral of John Speers. On that particular midday, the sky became thick with billowing clouds, which plunged the city into premature darkness. A spirit of great apprehension surged through the city of ten million. Everyone waited in an atmosphere charged with questions about God's judgment, or the Second Coming, or....

At 7:30 in the evening, I was standing in front of John's casket in a Filipino home, preaching a memorial service. Suddenly, as if a cosmic lever was released, Pinatubo's wrath began sprinkling noxious, acidic ash all over the city. It was an awesome, even frightening experience. Later, we rode for one and a half hours across the city in an open jeep, slowly making our way through the swirling discharge which had traveled in a cloud from the volcano sixty miles away. We put handkerchiefs over our noses and sat in deep reflection about God, nature, and power.

On October 19, (three months later) Julie and I traveled toward Pinatubo to personally view the havoc this giant had rained down upon millions. Soon we began to see ash piled up alongside the highway. Then cars came into view making their way through a shallow riverbed. The bridge had been cut by the force of the ash flow disgorged from the volcano. Mixed with rain, this material has come to be called *lahar*, which is like mud and follows the course of natural rivers.

We drove across the riverbed and on into Angeles, the city which had the dubious distinction of being the host city for the now abandoned American Clark Air Force Base. Dried *lahar* lined the streets while sandbags were piled in front of most buildings. Obviously the mud had overflowed the banks of nearby rivers and intruded throughout all the streets of one of the greatest sin cities of Asia. Bulldozers struggled valiantly to clear a path for cars through a riverbed right in the center of Angeles. Throughout the city, banners over the roads were swaying in the breeze, proclaiming, "Do not despair, Angeles will rise again;" "Lord Jesus, have mercy on us;" and "Mary, Mother of God, pray for us."

A few miles out of the city the road abruptly dropped 150 yards. A huge bridge was simply gone. Not a trace anywhere. Surrounding trees looked down on the *lahar*-covered fields with depression. Their once graceful limbs now drooped earthward. Along the road were baseball-sized *lahar* deposits which had been vomited violently out of the volcano.

In the distance Pinatubo stood in awesome victory. She seemed to mock the best efforts of man to control her fury. Crops were ruined. Fields of rich soil suffocated under five feet of ash. Hundreds of houses were buried. Refugee camps had sprung up in "safer areas." Over 500,000 people were displaced. Thousands were facing

201

starvation. Even today, the *lahar* continues to flow down the slopes of Pinatubo.

September, 1992

The sharp jangling of our bedside phone was an unwelcome intrusion into my deep 5:15 AM slumber. Groggily, I reached over, grabbed the instrument of discord and mumbled a less than cheery, "Hello." On the other end was a vibrant male voice giving me the announcement that he was from Zamboanga (the most violent city in the Philippines and one which is fraught with Christian-Muslim tensions). Greg Hapalla declared he would like to see me that very day. With a quick rush of adrenaline, I tried to figure out if this was a Muslim terrorist or, as he professed to be, a Muslim convert who hosted a radio program on the FEBC Christian station in Zamboanga. I sought to cross-check his credentials and finally agreed to meet him at our Reading Center that afternoon.

Zamboanga City is where the OM ship *Doulos* was docked in 1991, when a grenade was thrown into the middle of one of their meetings killing two, and injuring 35. Other bombings and killings have made this city a super tense place.

Greg did appear that afternoon and we had a delightful time together talking about how the Lord was using his daily, low-key, two-hour, extremely popular broadcast to Muslims. He told me of three death threats he had received, one of which I quote:

> *"You are the one who is God's curse because you are preaching the religion which is not true. When you die, you are going to Hell. If you will not stop your broadcast, this is your end. We will cut off your head and then we will hang it at Fort Pilar. This is the outcome of your preaching the religion which is Kafir.*
>
> —*The one who said this are the groups of the Mujahadin"*

Greg forcefully told me that he must continue to preach the Word of God regardless of the threats and danger to his life.

Twelve days later—4:15 PM. The phone rang again. This time one of the directors of FEBC was speaking, "Phil, I have very bad news for you. Three hours ago two Muslims walked into our station in Zamboanga and opened fire with 45 caliber pistols, killing Greg Hapalla who was broadcasting, along with radio technician Greg Bacabis and a Muslim bystander."

Within a few seconds, two very special men of God entered the roll of Christian martyrs and are today in the presence of our Lord. Greg Hapalla leaves behind a wife and three children in their late teens. Greg Bacabis was married with six children, some very young.

June, 1993

The formation of a consortium in 1984 of three missions—OMF, SEND, and SIM—was a dream fulfilled. We now would have the personnel and finances with which to make a significant evangelistic foray in and among the one million Magindanaon Muslims who reside on the southern island of Mindanao.

However, we all soon realized we were up against a massive foe which would not easily relinquish its vice-like grip on these people. Slowly, but surely, over the years, the team began to wear down. There was great frustration that came from the total lack of visible fruit. Fear was a normal reaction to omnipresent threats of violence. Physical problems abounded. Tensions began to create dissonance within the team. Small issues became inflated to the point of shattering relationships.

Spiritual correctives were emphasized. Retreats were conducted. A large team guest house provided a comfortable place for the children to play and enjoy one another. Adequate breaks were encouraged. Books on spiritual warfare were made available. Many hours were spent in individual counseling.

The results? Within nine years, the consortium was disbanded. Seventeen of the original 21 missionaries left the Magindanao outreach, fifteen of whom resigned from their respective missions. Of the original consortium group, only two couples, SIMers Dan and Nancy Rusch and Mark and Kathi Williams, remain working among this target people.   What does it take to murder a vision? More than the above! All three groups are still committed to seeing an evangelistic breakthrough among the Magindanao Muslims. Recruits and prayer support are being actively solicited, and some replacements are already on site.

Divine Threads Within A Human Tapestry

January – April, 1994

A few recorded reflections on our journey into the world of cancer.

January

In a few seconds our 747 will taxi down the Tokyo Narita airstrip commencing a 16 hour trip into Charlotte, NC. How eerily reminiscent of a moment eleven years ago when we sat on the same runway going through a similar crisis of perplexity and unsettledness. In both instances my briefcase held (and holds) a small slide of a biopsy that brazenly proclaims my precious wife of 32 years is a carrier of a serious malignant tumor. In the former instance, a ten day investigative process in the States revealed Julie to be a victim of no more than a lab mix up in her pathology report in Bangladesh.

Today, the chance of a rerun on that scenario is nil. While we were in New Haven, CT, in December Julie had some head congestion. Upon return to Manila, this condition soon worsened to the point of significant bleeding, including one memorable midnight session of blood flowing forth from her nose and mouth for an hour. For 21 long days we consulted a specialist (seven times) who treated her for a "sinus problem." Becoming increasingly apprehensive as the nose bleeds continued to flow on the average of once a day, we called Dr. Max Stevenson, the OMF doctor who had returned from New Zealand two days earlier. Immediately, he accompanied us to another Filipino specialist who, within five minutes, discovered a one-inch by half-inch tumor at the opening of Julie's Eustachian tube on the right side. The next day's fiber optic investigation and biopsy confirmed malignancy. All concerned agreed that an immediate medical evacuation to the States for treatment was imperative. It appears that chemotherapy and radiation will follow. We are told that, at this time, surgery cannot be performed because of the tumor's close proximity to the brain. We are thankful the bleeding has now stopped.

February

Very quickly upon arrival, we consulted with a top oncologist. The CAT scan taken here has revealed a Level 2 (on a scale of 4) fast spreading malignant tumor. It is highly treatable and has not spread to the bone or lymph nodes. Everything confirms the Manila report

The regimen of treatment prescribed is severe and, for this type of cancer, should have a 90 percent total cure rate. Julie will start right away with (1) radiation five days a week for seven weeks, and (2) a severe high-reaction CIS Platinum chemotherapy, "the strongest there is," that will require Julie to go into the hospital overnight for its introduction into the system. There will be two 21 day cycles of this treatment. The first 10-12 days of each 21 days will be tough.

Why so much so fast? Our doctor says this is the only way to maximize the treatment and obtain the highest cure rate. We agree and are ready for the harsh days ahead. Above all, we long for the "all clear" and we will fight together to get to that point. If all goes perfectly, which basically means Julie can keep the treatment going and the tumor shrinks, then around 3 ½ months should see us through the tunnel that lies before us.

April

Somewhere between the 4th and 5th floor of the Charlotte Presbyterian Hospital, I turned to the middle-aged lady in the elevator and said, "Oh, I see you are going to the 6th floor. What's there?" She joyfully responded, "That's obstetrics." Then I commented, "That is a happy place. I'm going up one to the cancer floor." It was as if I shot her with a pistol. Her face grimaced with pain as she stuttered, "Oh, I'm sorry, so very sorry. I'm so sorry." And then the elevator door clanked open into a world of beaming mothers and sighing babies taking their first breaths in their new world of life and hope.

Seconds later, I was exiting into a surrealistic world of death and hopelessness. Zombie-like aged patients lay prostrate in pain, locked into thoughts of their soon exit into eternity. Certain doors are plastered with signs prohibiting entry into rooms in which the patients have become temporarily radioactive through implants. Shuffling down the halls, with their IV drip stands in tow, are the living dead.

In the midst of this scene of despair are the "angels of mercy" like we have never seen anywhere. There are no words to describe the beautiful people we have met, both doctors and nurses, during this sojourn of pain. How can they consistently be so sensitive, caring, affirming, and loving? It was a humbling experience to be placed in their gentle hands of grace. Truly, they have a special calling, and they are fulfilling it overwhelmingly well.

How grateful we are that Julie's condition was not as serious as most of the other cancer patients. She was required to take the two doses of CIS Platinum chemotherapy. I was able to be with her the whole time. At one point, just after the second chemo, she took a massive nose dive and became as near an Alzheimer's patient as I ever want to see her! For five days she was "out of it." They put her back in the hospital for 24 hours of rehydration and medicine through IV drips. This was a great help, though weakness and three times daily vomiting have continued throughout the whole time.

Julie's radiation went on for seven weeks and totaled 35 treatments. Quite a bit of radiation burn has discolored her neck and sides of her face. Her throat has been very sore, making it difficult to swallow. She has lost 13 pounds. Actually, the only ongoing negative from the treatment will be a permanent loss of saliva with subsequent dry mouth.

And now, for the super good news. Yesterday, both our oncologist and radiologist gave Julie the all clear. The tumor is gone! The two slightly swollen lymph nodes are now normal. She will have a CAT-scan in six weeks or so, but it is expected to confirm the fiber optic exam. The doctors have approved our plans to return to Manila July 26. They said she should be up to 90 percent normal strength by then. What a moment of rejoicing. We went to the hospital snack shop to celebrate and both went into the restroom. I shouted hallelujah... and Julie threw up! Well, each to his or her own way to throw a celebration.

Reflection

Is there ever a conclusion to adversity while we are robed in our bodies of vulnerable flesh? Sorry, but no. We must all concur with Paul's biological insight, "I die daily." And while in that mode of deterioration, all kinds of painful realities jar us out of complacency. It may be our illness or someone else's. Tragedy may suddenly strike a loved one. A natural disaster may wipe out thousands.

And we sit back and ponder. Why her? Why me? Why now? Why at all? For some, the crucible strengthens faith. For others, it destroys faith.

So how do I conclude this difficult and even heart wrenching chapter? Oh, there is comfort. No, not escape, but comfort. Jesus promises a paradox to the buffeted believer. Peace in the raging storm. Consolation in perplexity. Companionship in loneliness. Hope within hopelessness.

Now, what about that tapestry? Never far from my consciousness there rings an incessant, clarion call, "FINISH THE TAPESTRY, FINISH THE TAPESTRY." Even though its final form may look a bit tattered and worn; some of the threads may have wandered a little off course; colors may be somewhat faded; still, there can be a finished wholeness, an honorable completeness; yes, a product that reflects the ringing affirmation of the Apostle Paul's words of farewell to the Ephesian elders (with the alteration of but one word).

I consider my life worth nothing to me, if only I may finish the tapestry *the Lord Jesus has given to me* (Acts 20:24)

A Final Word

The question might be asked, "Has it all been worthwhile?" That indeed is a legitimate query.

But let me extrapolate a bit. Does the postman who has faithfully delivered mail door to door for 30 years feel that his life has "made a difference?" Have the sore feet and aching bones been worth the expended effort? How about the dodging of unleashed pit bulls? Then there is always the metamorphosis of the blazing sun to the pelting rain, and on to the driving blizzard. Does the postman's job satisfaction involve any more than a regular salary with substantial benefits?

How about the executive saleswoman? She is hawking a worthy product. But is her sales motivation anything other than her desire to obtain a hefty commission? Would she, for instance, die for her product's sales success? Doubtful.

So, I survey the endless variety of ways to put in 40 hours in order to keep one's body and soul united as a cohesive whole. Each option has its plusses and minuses.

But what really is the bottom line for my life? Is it financial security? Should the focus be on having a comfortable and enjoyable lifestyle? How about freedom from fear concerning the safety of my family? These and many other issues can claim a measure of legitimacy in regard to the expenditure of my time and talents.

I, however, keep coming back to a few key Scriptures verses:

The words of Christ, *"If anyone would come after me, he must deny himself and take up his cross and follow me. For whoever wants to save his life will lose it, but whoever loses his life for me and for the gospel will save it. What good is it for a man to gain the whole world yet forfeit his soul?"* Mark 8:34-36.

These powerful exhortations, which demand total commitment, moved me in the direction of the Muslim world. How can the Church of Jesus Christ ignore the spiritual needs of the 1.2 billion who are lost and destined to spend eternity without Christ? Islam, numerically, is second only to Christianity. It is one of the world's three monotheistic religions, the third being Judaism. With the help of Arab oil money, Islam is now engaged in effective and widespread propagation of its beliefs. It is the world's fastest growing religion; due mainly to the propensity of Muslims to have large families.

When Julie and I responded to the call for involvement in missions, there was only one missionary for every million Muslims. Today that figure is not as extreme. Still, Islam represents the largest unreached people group in the world. In many areas, they are the most resistant.

But as I read the Great Commission, I see no exceptions. The Gospel is for all of mankind. Muslims must be lovingly confronted with the Christian alternative. And that, at whatever cost to the one doing the presentation.

To the question, "Has it all been worthwhile?" comes a resounding positive response. I cannot imagine any other direction of life that could have possibly been as fulfilling, joyful, or satisfying as that which I have chosen.

And, so, the "final word" is simply an invitation to the reader to prayerfully consider a commitment to involvement in the Muslim world.

"Oh, that the world of Islam may taste and see that the Lord is good."